A Guide to
Chicago and Midwestern
POLISH-AMERICAN
GENEALOGY

By

Jason Kruski

CLEARFIELD

Published for Clearfield Company by
Genealogical Publishing Company
Baltimore, Maryland
2012

ISBN 978-0-8063-5577-1

Made in the United States of America

CONTENTS

INTRODUCTION

The idea for this book came when I was engaged in a genealogical discussion with some fellow researchers. Although there are many books about general genealogical research, I realized there was no tome written for the Polish–Americans of the Midwest and, specifically, the Chicagoland area. Some books are written on Polish–American genealogy, and some books specifically focus on Chicago research. However, no books have combined the two. I decided this situation needed fixing, because Chicago has been the historic stronghold of Polish–Americans. Poles came to Chicago for the opportunities it offered and then scattered across the Midwest and the United States. Millions of Americans today can trace some line of ancestry back to the Polish population of Cook County.

Chicago has been the home to Poles since its beginning in the 1830s, and it continues to have a large Polish population. A short drive down Chicago's Milwaukee Avenue reveals Polish store signs and other advertisements mixed in with signs in English, Spanish, and many other languages. Some with a serious interest in genealogy founded the Polish Genealogical Society of America (PGSA), which continues to grow and expand each year.

I've always had an interest in history, and I occasionally asked older relatives about family history. I began casually researching my grandparents and other known family members approximately ten years ago. My serious interest in genealogy began when my great-aunt died approximately four years ago. Now that I am older, I regret not asking my relatives more questions while they were alive, because I realize they could have produced a much more vibrant family tree than what I have found through my research. Sadly, we cannot turn back the clock, so instead we push forward and determine how to piece the past back together from what is left today.

This book focuses on the years 1860 to 1945, and the target ancestry group is Polish Catholics. Jewish/Lithuanian/Ruthenian ancestry will not be covered, because the other groups living in Poland deserve their own books and strategies for research. The majority of Jews in Poland lived in urban areas in contrast to the majority of Polish Catholics who lived in the countryside and worked as farmers. While the style of recordkeeping did overlap across religions in nineteenth century Poland, it would not be fair to lump Jewish records into a book that is mostly about Polish Catholic Church records. The Polish–Lithuanian Commonwealth stretched, at its height, from the Baltic Sea to the Black Sea and encompassed countless lands, peoples, and cultures. To make this guide practical, its focus is on Poland as defined by its boundaries today, not five hundred years ago.

This book can also help people of German ancestry who lived in Poland throughout the centuries but only if those Germans were Catholics who freely mixed with the Poles in their communities. Most Germans stayed within their Lutheran communities, but some did mix freely. Often, Lutherans attended the Catholic churches in their regions and were recorded as such in church books. Persons of German–Polish descent should consult Polish sources as well as German sources for genealogical information.

Genealogy is a wonderful hobby for people of all ages, and with the explosion of information available on the Internet, it is easier today than ever before. Anyone can research their family's history. A lot of this research can be done at home using websites such as www.ancestry.com and www.familysearch.com, which have searchable databases with millions of historic images just waiting to give up their information.

This book is for the modern genealogist—someone who searches extensively via the Internet. Technology has revolutionized so many different fields that it is only appropriate that genealogists embrace it as well. This book shows how much easier genealogical research has become in recent years.

Now, I said easier—not easy. Whoever said that genealogy is easy probably has a family Bible that records the names of all their ancestors back to American colonial times. People who possess that should consider themselves very lucky, because most people do not. Unfortunately, very few Poles kept records in this manner.

Many people do not research their Polish genealogy because they do not speak the language. Polish genealogy books I have read emphasize how important learning Polish is for genealogical research. Well, I'm going to break with tradition and say you absolutely do not need to learn Polish to research your Polish roots. Granted, it is a major plus, but it is not a necessity.

The majority of church records were kept in Latin in Poland, so knowledge of English will help more than knowledge of Polish. Of the vital records written in Polish, it is only necessary to learn a basic vocabulary of two dozen words along with the basic numbers and months. I am not fluent in Polish, but I can easily read the Polish vital records for my ancestors. Flip to Chapter Ten to read more about the role of the Polish language in Polish genealogy.

I will supplement the information in this book with personal stories about my ancestors. My family is not extraordinary; I consider my ancestors to be quite ordinary Poles. However, it is in their ordinariness that they become perfect for a volume like this; they can speak for the others of their generations who came to America looking for freedom in the 1880s or 1900s in ways that the noblemen who fled Poland in the 1830s cannot. Their stories are the stories of millions of Poles who came to America looking for a better life.

One important note about this book is that it is not an encyclopedia or textbook of any kind. This is an original analysis that I have created from the sources available to the Polish–American researcher. Therefore, all opinions, ratings, and ideas are mine alone and in no way, shape, or form represent the official stances of any of the agencies mentioned in this book. The history in this book is kept to a minimum, because I urge you to research the history that your unique ancestors experienced. You can find much more definitive guides on these specific subjects elsewhere.

The use of abbreviations is minimal, but there are two important abbreviations used in this book. Instead of writing out "great-great-grandparents" every time, I will abbreviate the word great with the letter g, so gg would mean great-great, ggg great-great-great, and so on. "LDS" stands for Latter-Day Saints—as in the Church of Latter-Day Saints, the Mormon Church. The LDS church is committed to the genealogy of all people around the globe, regardless of religion or race. Therefore, during the past few decades, LDS members have microfilmed and digitally photographed records of great importance to the Cook County Polish. The fruits of their labor can be accessed via their website, www.familysearch.org or via microfilm in a family history library that LDS has established. These are found across the United States and in many other countries as well.

In short, I am honored that you are reading my book. I wish you the best in your family history search, and I invite you to contact me at kruskij@gmail.com if you have any comments about the content in this book.

Best wishes,

Jason Kruski

CHAPTER ONE: THE FIRST STEPS

Before a hiker hits the trails of a national park, he or she needs to consult a map or guide of some kind. The same is true of genealogy. Before beginning genealogical research, a basic family tree needs to be constructed from the information easily found in your home or from relatives. The map for genealogy does not contain mileage or landmarks; it contains names, dates, and other pertinent information that can guide research backward in time.

To begin your research, just from memory, sketch a pedigree chart. To draw a family tree, start with yourself and then work backward. Write your name, birthday, marriage day, spouse and children's names, etc. That's easy. Now do the same for your parents. At the minimum, write their full names, birthdays, and date of marriage. Now write your grandparents' information.

Also write where all of this happened. This is important. The location of these crucial events tells everything about who your ancestors were along with some insight into why they may have made the life decisions that they did. Many Poles did not come directly to Cook County; my great-grandfather Wojciech Gabrys lived in Pennsylvania and Michigan before eventually arriving in Chicago in the late 1910s. I researched a friend's line whose direct ancestor was born in West Virginia, but that ancestor's siblings were born in Illinois. Writing any family stories that involve states other than Illinois can pay off in the end, so make a note even if you are unsure whether it actually happened.

Finding your grandparents' information may have been difficult, but finding information about their parents and grandparents is even harder. Write all the information that you can find about your grandparents' ancestry. Even if all you know are rumors or ideas, write it and put it in their file. Maybe there's a story about gg-granddaddy marrying an Irish woman. Usually these stories have a grain of truth, so write everything you know. (Maybe his wife had red hair, so her nickname was the Irish woman?)

Exhaust your mind and the resources easily at your disposal to come up with that pedigree. Sift through old papers and possessions that may have belonged to relatives and ancestors. After doing that, consult other family members who are either interested in family history or are older and may have known the people that you wrote down. Usually families have someone interest in genealogy, be it your father or that distant cousin you've only seen twice. Look up their information, contact them, and talk to them.

To produce the best family tree possible, meeting and talking with others is absolutely necessary. Genealogy is a team sport. Solo genealogical research is possible, but you will miss out on a wealth of information by not tapping all possible relatives for family history information. Everyone's memory is different, and they may help you in ways that you or your parents cannot.

Search for documents that may be in your house or the house of a relative. Ask your mother/aunt/grandmother/older relative if you could look through their old papers and pictures to find family history information. Try to find birth certificates, marriage records, and other documents that give genealogically significant information. This information includes the date of an event such as a birth, baptism, or marriage; the place of an event; or the names of cousins/siblings/other relatives.

What If I Don't Have Any Known Relatives Who Know About Family History?

Welcome to my life. Almost all of my relatives who knew family history are dead or had poor memories by the time I reached them. This is the entire reason why I wrote this book. Traditional Polish genealogy books revel in having the *babcia* who can tell you all about the old country. Maybe you are like me and didn't know what a *babcia* was until the genealogical quest began. In case you were wondering, it is Polish for "grandmother" and is pronounced boo-sha in its affectionate form.

Therefore, a more pragmatic approach to genealogy is needed. Don't despair; there are relatives out there who are interested in family history. The tricky part is finding them. Consult Chapter Fourteen for tips on how to locate living relatives who may work with you on your quest.

What If I Am Adopted?

Illinois recently passed a law that birth information must be provided to adoptees who request it if they were born before 1946. I recommend that you research this law and its implications before using it. More information about this law and other adoption laws can be found at http://www.newillinoisadoptionlaw.com/

Adoption research can be tricky. Genealogists cannot go simply based on shared names or surnames to discover ancestry. After all, there are thousands of John Nowak's out there. Finding a vital record that proves descent from a particular individual is critical. Not all adoptees can do this. The best thing is to find out as much about the adopted ancestor as possible and then research possible orphanages or people at that time and place.

If absolute worst comes to worst, and no information about birth parents can be found from the state or relatives, then there is only one hope left. Skip to Chapter Thirteen and try genetic genealogy as a means to find someone who shares DNA segments with you. People have found relatives using this route. It is not easy, but it is definitely worth a shot.

Assembling all that information may have been easy but probably was rather difficult. Now that information needs to be stored and organized so it is easy to access, use, and share. I cringe when I see others at genealogy gatherings carrying around massive binders filled with papers and notebooks containing massive pedigree charts. In this day and age, do not do genealogy with a paper and pencil.

Today, computers are so powerful and have so many features that you should do yourself a favor by purchasing family history software. Granted, there are several free family tree programs available on the Internet and one need only type "free family tree software" into Google to find them. However, the best family history software comes at a price.

I recommend Family Tree Maker published by the genealogical giant, Ancestry.com. Ancestry is the bread and butter of every genealogist who has ancestry in the United States, and their software is excellent. It is reliable and can store and backup massive amounts of information. Users can build virtual family trees, attach documents to people, generate charts and reports, and more. It is relatively expensive but worth it.

Another great feature that this software has is that it connects to www.ancestry.com automatically as information is keyed into the software in order to help you to find documents and information relating to your particular ancestors.

That being said, doing a thorough search of the resources in your home and the homes of relatives is a must before delving into the realm of genealogy. All kinds of sources of information can hide in relatives' attics and basements. Researching like this in the beginning will save a time and prevent confusion in the long run.

That was a lot of work, but I hope you found good preliminary information and now have it organized. Now the fun begins—traveling back in time to find those ancestors!

CHAPTER TWO: U.S. CENSUS RECORDS

The next step after uncovering family papers and gathering memories is sifting through materials available in the rest of the world, mainly via the Internet. After piecing together what you know about your family, it is now time to back up this information with official documents.

The first document to use is the U.S. census undertaken by the federal government to count the population of its citizens. This collection of federal records is a wealth of information. The U.S. government has taken a census of the population once every ten years, beginning in 1790.

The kind of information found on census records depends on the year it was taken. The census did not begin naming wives and children until 1850, and it was not until the 1900 census that a year of immigration was documented. That being said, there is still much information perfect for genealogy to be found in the records. Lucky for genealogists, census records have been microfilmed and digitized and thus preserved for future generations.

For Polish Chicagoans, the main timeframe of usefulness for census records is from the 1870 census through the 1930 census. The 1860 census will be useful to the Panna Maria Poles in Texas, but before that census year, few Poles can be found. Census records become public information 72 years after they were enumerated, so the 1940 census will become available for researchers to use in 2012. The 1950 census will be available in 2022 and so on.

Sadly, the 1890 census was burnt to a crisp in a fire in a government warehouse. There are some fragments available from certain parts of the country, but no returns from Cook County survived.

Why Are Census Records Special?

Census records are beautiful pieces of information, because they provide snapshots of a particular family once every ten years. They show who was living with whom, occupations, vital data like birth and marriage years, and other useful information.

Finding your ancestors in census records is critical, because they provide addresses, give clues as to when children were born/married/died, and in general provide a greater picture for your family. What kind of neighborhood did they live in? Did they live in the Back of the Yards and work as butchers at the Union Stockyards? Did they live on Noble Street next to Stanislaus Kostka Church? Were they unemployed? Did they get remarried after the death of a spouse? All of this information can be found in census records.

The longer your ancestor was in the United States, the more likely they are to appear in the census. If your ancestor came to the United States in 1909 or 1910, then he or she probably will not show up in the 1910 census simply because they would have been so new to the country and therefore probably had not purchased property or married. If a person owned a home, then the odds of he or she being in that particular census are very good.

Boarders often do not show up in the records. A married couple with children is more likely to appear than a single person who just came from a foreign country. A good strategy is to begin searching for an ancestor in the last census they were counted in before he or she died and then work backward. The 1930 census is excellent; I have found every person I looked for with one exception. That is compared to dozens of "missing people" in the 1880 and 1900 census. Start recently, and then work backward.

Finding Census Records

Census records are found on many different genealogical websites. I recommend www.ancestry.com, because it is the largest Internet genealogy company with the best census indexes to search. Ancestry has all federal censuses indexed with images ready to view. A paid subscription is required to see the information on this site, but it is worth the money for someone starting out in genealogy or planning to greatly expand a branch or two of his or her family tree.

What is useful about finding census records on Ancestry is that other members can correct information that was either transcribed incorrectly into the database or written incorrectly in the image. This can be useful for others trying to find those people. I have corrected all incorrect spellings of my ancestors and any neighbors I have come across to help people find them more easily. Few employees at Ancestry are familiar with the Polish language, so transcription errors are common.

Issues with Finding Ancestry in the Census Records

In addition to transcription errors, original documents will contain a multitude of other errors. This is because of a combination of census takers with poor handwriting, ancestors' thick accents, and the fact that many census takers did not know the Polish alphabet or Polish spelling customs. Usually the longer people have been in America, the easier it is to find them in the census, probably because they have learned more and more about the English language and have either Anglicized their Polish names or are used to spelling out names like "Wojciech" for non-Polish people.

This phenomenon is not restricted to names; all kinds of information probably will be wrong on census records. The information is generally close but rarely 100-percent accurate. I made a spreadsheet of my ancestors' information in the beginning of my research just to figure out their names and years of immigration based upon census records. I got 1875, 1877, and 1880 for my gg-grandmother. The actual year was 1874.

The same is true of birthdays. Women's birth years generally will be a year or two younger than their actual age. Some of this is because of vanity. My great-grandmother always gave her birth year as 1892 when, in fact, her baptism record proves that she was really born in 1891. Some of this was because of poor English skills and difficulty in saying the year in English.

Also keep in mind that your ancestor may or may not have been home when the census taker knocked on the door. This information may have been given to the taker by someone who lived with him or her or by a neighbor. That person may have guessed approximately 50 for your ancestor's age when he or she was really 46 or 47. The census takers did not wait around for people to return; they wrote the information down as best as they could and moved on to the next house.

What If I Can't Find My Ancestor in a Census?

Flip to Appendix B for tips on how to find a Polish ancestor in an Internet database. Polish people don't have it as easy as the English, Irish, or Scottish who spoke English as a native language and thus are more easily (and accurately) recorded in census records.

Make sure the ancestors in question actually were in the country during the census year. Knowing approximately when they originally came to America is a big help. Sometimes Poles went back to Poland for brief stretches of time. My great-grandfather Stanislaw Stelmach returned to Poland in the late 1910s and was not in the 1920 census because he was in Poland then.

Immigration and emigration records will tell this type of information. Flip to Chapter Four for information about finding an ancestor's immigration documents. Some people may have arrived in a census year but missed being counted because censuses were taken months before their arrival. My great-grandfather's brother arrived in the United States in September 1910 and thus was not found in the 1910 census.

Finding a House in the Census

If the address of the person in question is known, another strategy is to locate that home in the census records to see who was living in the house at the time. Sometimes your ancestor will not be listed at that address, because he or she was a boarder so the census taker didn't think to ask about anyone else living in that house.

Now, finding a particular house in the census is a relatively complicated process, because the censuses were divided up based on their own enumeration districts, not based on wards or districts of Chicago. Determining which enumeration district that house was in is vital for searching with this method. Luckily www.stevemorse.com is an excellent resource for determining that elusive enumeration district. Unfortunately, this can only be completely done for the 1900, 1920, and 1930 censuses. Morse and his volunteers are working on 1940. Addresses from the 1880 census cannot be found using this site.

The Chicago street-numbering system was changed for residential areas in 1909, so a person could have been living in the same house in 1900 and 1910, but the address will be different in the census records. Street names have also changed over time. A resource for converting old addresses to new addresses and vice versa can be found on Chicago Ancestors, a website run by the Newberry Library of Chicago: http://chicagoancestors.org/#tab-tools

Once the exact address is known, find a map of Chicago. Many can be found on the Internet. To find the enumeration district for a house in the 1900 census, an old map of Chicago will be needed. Search for the major streets around where your ancestor lived, and find them in the enumeration district definitions on Stephen Morse's site at http://www.stephenmorse.com/census/index.html

Simply click on Illinois – Chicago – and then click on at least two major streets in the area of your ancestor's house. The best method is to note the four major streets surrounding the house in question. That will give the precise enumeration district that the address will be in.

Once the enumeration district is found, go back to Ancestry, click on the card catalog, click on the census in question, click on the state and city, and finally click on the enumeration district that house was located in. Then sift through the images until that address is found.

Again, that is a long process, but if it helps to find an ancestor, then it will be well worth the effort. Some census documents are so illegible that searching for the address is the only way to find that family.

Other Census Documents

Aside from the normal census documents, there were other schedules made by census takers that enumerated things such as farming and industry. One such schedule that will be helpful to Poles in Cook County is the mortality schedule that was enumerated for the 1850–1880 censuses. A mortality schedule is a census listing all of the people who died in the twelve months before the day that census taker came to the house. This is useful because few Polish churches kept death records before the 1880s in Cook County. I found a stillborn child from my gg-grandparents in the 1880 mortality schedule that I would not have known about without that schedule. In fact, the information is cross-referenced; the number that the family was given on the proper census form is used on the mortality schedule as well.

Farming schedules are useful for ancestry in southern Illinois or in other rural parts of the Midwest. These do not contain much genealogical information, but they help tell more about that person's life in ways that vital records do not. They tell what kind of farmer that person was, how much land was owned, and more

Other Sites with Searchable Databases of Census Records

If your ancestor cannot be found in Ancestry census records, then try other databases. Remember, other places employed other transcribers who may have had greater eyesight or more knowledge of Polish and thus could transcribe the records better. The Church of Latter Day Saints (LDS) website—www.familysearch.org—is rapidly adding census records to its databases and will catch up some day in terms of size and scope to Ancestry. The main difference between Family Search and Ancestry is that Ancestry requires a paid subscription to use its databases whereas Family Search is free.

The drawback to Family Search is that not all census databases have images attached to them. At the time of this writing, only the 1870 and 1900 censuses have images that are freely searchable whereas the other censuses have only the transcribed information available to search without the accompanying images. Seeing the original records is a must for genealogists. These transcriptions can point the way to the originals but are no substitutes for the real documents.

Another searchable database that has some census images is www.Fold3.com. A paid subscription is needed to access the images on Fold3, but its databases can be searched for free. Also, many public libraries subscribe to www.heritagequest.com and their patrons can access the census records transcribed on that website. Ask a reference librarian at your local public library for more information about research with Heritage Quest.

Conclusion

In general, the larger the household, the easier it is to find them in the census. If the parents are nowhere to be found, then search for their children. That is how I found my gg-grandparents in the 1910 census. I had no luck with "Michael Pietrzak" or even "Constance Pietrzak." Then I tried searching for my ancestor, their daughter, Agnes Pietrzak. Bingo. I found her and her family. My ancestors were transcribed as "Michel Retzok and Clara Retzok." I couldn't find anything on Michael because his age was given as 48, quite an achievement considering he was listed as 45 in the 1900 census (he was actually born in 1854). My ancestor Agnes was spelled normally so I was able to find her via that route.

Creative searching is a must with Polish–American genealogy. Too often have I found people discouraged that they cannot find their ancestors just by simply typing in their names or some common variations. If you can't find your ancestor by typing in Michal, Michael, Mike, or even Mikal, do not get discouraged. Our ancestors were struggling to learn English and to fit in this country. Providing clear and accurate information to the census taker was not of enormous importance. If you cannot find your ancestors, flip to appendix B for tips on how to find Polish names in American sources.

That being said, census information is usually good—just take it with a grain of salt and let it be a guide to find the original documents that prove the information in it. A true genealogist cannot take any one source for granted. He or she needs to find as many sources as possible to verify information. To verify the ages and birth information given in the census records, the next step is to find the vital records of our ancestors.

CHAPTER THREE: U.S. VITAL RECORDS

After exhausting census records, the next step is to determine the exact dates of births, marriages, and deaths for your ancestors. This information is found in vital records, the official records of births, marriages, and deaths that occurred in a certain municipality. This section covers vital records in Cook County, Illinois. For vital records in Poland, skip to Chapter Eleven. The first section of this chapter covers the government's vital records for Poles. The second section covers the vital information found in church records.

Section 1: State

A. Births

Beginning in 1877, Illinois mandated that births be recorded. In 1878, Cook County began issuing birth certificates. Some records were kept before this in the form of birth registers, which exist from 1871 to 1915. If you have Polish–American ancestry in Cook County, do not expect to find all of your ancestors' and extended family's birth certificates. It does not matter that most Poles were born after record keeping became mandatory for physicians and midwives in Illinois. Record keeping simply did not reach the state's entire population. And those records that were kept were often sloppily written, so finding them in their respective collections can be difficult.

Virtually all vital records for Chicago were destroyed in the Great Chicago Fire in 1871, so 1871 is generally the starting point for government documents in Cook County. Record keeping got better and better as the years wore on, but it did not get close to recording 100 percent of the population until about the early 1930s.

A typical state-issued birth certificate issued between 1878 and 1916 will have the child's name on it along with his or her gender, race, date of birth, how many children that mother had to date, address of birth, parents' names, parents' birthplaces, parents' ages, mother's maiden name, occupation of father, and information about the attendant who completed the certificate. Both birth certificates and birth registers have this information. The difference between the two is that the certificate is one piece of paper that only lists information about the person in question versus the register, which was kept in a large ledger book, extended to two pages, and contained information about many people on those two pages in a columnar format.

Most Polish–Americans delivered babies via midwife. Only the wealthier Poles gave birth in hospitals. If the mother was seriously ill or if there was a complication during the pregnancy, then a doctor was called in to attend to the birth. Few of the early Poles' birth certificates are signed by a doctor. Doctors generally were more detailed and thorough with record-keeping than midwives were, so birth certificates filled out by doctors yield more information. Believe it or not, but doctors' handwriting tended to be neater and more legible than most people's handwriting.

From 1916 onward, the information is mostly the same. The difference is that after 1916, a new, cleaner form was used that allowed for greater precision and detailed information. Post-1916 records are very legible and usually contain more details about the parents' birthplaces. They still tend to only list the country of birth of the parent (if born outside of the United States), but sometimes they do contain more information.

The Cook County Clerk's office is the master repository of Cook County vital records. One can obtain copies of birth certificates and birth registers in a number of different ways, which are all detailed on the Cook County Clerk website: http://www.cookcountyclerk.com/vitalrecords/Pages/default.aspx

The Clerk's website boasts that you can get copies of vital records in many different manners, but that only applies to recent vital records (their main business). For genealogical purposes, complete the form on that page and mail it with a check or money order.

The Cook County Clerk's office has a genealogical website that contains searchable databases and links to purchase copies of the original documents at http://www.cookcountygenealogy.com/

This website has the potential to be a good resource. The advantage of this website is that downloading a scan of the record can be done almost instantaneously rather than waiting weeks for it to arrive in the mail. The disadvantage is that it costs $15 plus a convenience fee for using a credit card, which is not ideal for someone who is researching family history and will need probably dozens of birth records. Generally, the more recent the birth certificate, the more likely it is to be found on the website. The keyers at the Clerk's office started with the early 1930s and are moving backward.

The best resource for finding these records is the LDS website at www.familysearch.org. The volunteer indexers finished keying the Cook County birth records a while ago, and the images, along with the completed index, are free. This is the resource that I used to find all the birth certificates and birth register entries for my ancestors. The indexes are very good to use (and I'm not saying that because I helped to key them!). The handwriting before 1916 is poor on most records, and many birth registers are ripped or missing ends of the pages. Therefore, finding your ancestors in them will be tricky. Do not give up hope—it can be done. It just takes persistence and creativity.

Another useful technique is to browse the images. Sometimes indexers didn't transcribe the person's name correctly. Sometimes the original document has incorrect spelling. Sometimes the document is unreadable and the average indexer cannot spend a long time deciphering what an unusual name says. Stuff happens. That is when browsing through the specific images that your ancestors might be in is a useful strategy.

Browsing through the birth registers is a lot more efficient than the birth certificates, because every child listed in the birth register had a birth certificate of some kind, usually with the exact same information. The difference is that one may have been indexed correctly whereas the other was not, so be sure to check both. The disappointing thing is that the registers ended in 1915, so they are only a useful source of birth information between 1871 and 1915.

Another useful resource is the Cook County delayed-birth index. Delayed-birth records were issued by a government in order to provide documentation to people whose births were not recorded at the moment of the event, for one reason or another. This collection has been published on neither the Cook County Clerk's website nor the LDS website. It can only be accessed via microfilm at a LDS Family History library. See Chapter Seven for more information about delayed-birth records.

In my experience, I have found that birth reporting was much better on the North Side of Chicago than on the South Side. I found my family's earliest birth records from the early 1880s on the North Side. I have found no birth records for my South Side family in the 1880s. The first few I have for South Side Poles were from the mid-1890s. The 1870s generally did not have good record-keeping on either side of the city. I haven't found any birth records for the 1870s for my Polish family.

Birth recording was decent in the 1890s and 1900s. It was good for the 1910s, but it was not until the 1920s that I would deem it excellent. It wasn't until the late 1930s and 1940s that birth recording covered virtually all of Illinois' population. I have found most of my ancestors after 1900, but there are still some who elude me. Why didn't their births get recorded? It is difficult to say.

Another incentive for finding birth records in Cook County is that they almost always included the address of birth for that child. That is a valuable piece of information, because many Poles moved from house to house in the late 1800s. Keeping a record of their homes helps to find them in census records and identify previously unknown children. It can also help to verify who the person was in a death certificate, but that is getting ahead of the game.

B. Marriage Licenses and Applications

For me, marriage records are the happiest genealogical records to research. Death records are sad by nature, and birth records are often sad too considering that many of those children died in childhood. A marriage record proves that a relative survived to adulthood, got married, and maybe had a few children. Unfortunately, state-issued marriage certificates are the least informative resource for Cook County research.

Marriage certificates can be found in Cook County from 1871 until now. There are few pre-1871 marriage certificates in existence. Some clues to these vital records can be found using Sam Fink's index at

http://www.cyberdriveillinois.com/departments/archives/fink.html

Sam Fink wanted to reconstruct marriage records that were destroyed in the Great Chicago Fire, so he compiled a list of marriages based on information he found in newspaper archives. There are few Poles in this collection, but it is worth a shot nonetheless.

Marriage records are by far the easiest of the vital records to find in Cook County, because they are the most complete form of vital record keeping that exists there. I have found a marriage license for every single couple in my Cook County family tree that got married there, stretching from my gg-grandparents in 1874 down to my grandparents in 1958.

Why was record-keeping so good for marriage licenses? Well, there had to be a license in place in the county building before a priest could perform a ceremony. He would not marry a couple unless they had been to city hall, gotten a license, and were allowed to be lawfully wed. That is why searching for marriage licenses in Cook County is so easy.

Again, original copies of these documents can be obtained from the Cook County Clerk via mail or their website. The website mostly has records from the 1930s through the early 1960s, so it is useful for recent genealogical searching but not for historic marriages.

By far, the two best sources of marriage information are the LDS website and the website of the Illinois Secretary of State: www.cyberdriveillinois.com. The Secretary of State site has many excellent databases that can be searched for vital records. One of the most useful is the Illinois marriage index. Cook County is included from 1871 to April 1901 along with Sam Fink's index of pre-1871 marriages.

The advantage to using this website is that it automatically uses the "begins with" method of searching. In other words, typing in "Stefan" produces every surname beginning with "Stefan." This is a useful feature for Polish–Americans who often got their names butchered in these vital records. I found Valentine Stefaniak by typing in "Stefan" and getting "Stefanok, Walentin" as my result. Interestingly enough, my gg-grandmother's name was written backward on the actual record so that her name was transcribed as "Katarizina, Josefa" instead of Jozwiak, Katherina as it should have been. My jaw dropped when I found this record.

After finding an ancestor in the Secretary of State database, get a copy of the original marriage license from the LDS website using their free database. The transcriptions done by volunteers for the state of Illinois are fairly close to the LDS transcriptions, so type in what the Secretary of State's database said and the record should pop up easily. If not, then try the search tricks outlined in Appendix B. If a record is in the Secretary of State database, then it definitely can be found on the LDS website, so keep at it until you've got that record in your hands … err, I mean your hard drive.

Marriage licenses do not tell much, but they do give three key pieces of information: the marriage date, the ages of the bride and groom, and where the marriage took place. The clerk at city hall completed the top portion of the license, but the bottom portion was completed by the parish priest. Generally, the names on the bottom of the license are written more clearly and spelled correctly, because they were written by a Polish-speaking priest rather than an English-speaking clerk. It is unfortunate that the indexes were done based on the top part of the license.

That being said, the bottom part still probably won't be completely accurate. For the marriage I mentioned above, the groom and bride were listed on the bottom of their marriage license respectively as Valentin Stefanek and Catarina Juzwiok—closer to their actual names but still not quite there.

The top part includes the names of the bride and groom and where they lived (almost always it just says Chicago or Cook County.) It also includes their ages, which are usually pretty accurate. Finally, the date the license was issued will be there.

The bottom part includes the names again, but it also includes the date of the actual marriage, the name of the priest or minister presiding over the marriage, and where the marriage took place. This is a crucial piece of information, because knowing the church that your ancestors got married in paves the way in finding more records about that couple, particularly children's baptism records. Also, church marriage records are more detailed than civil marriage records, so a civil marriage record is very useful for finding the church's record.

Marriage applications are a different matter for every other county in Illinois—Cook County is the oddball. Always funny how that works out, right? For most other counties, a separate form called a marriage application was completed. It contained all kinds of rich genealogical data, such as the names of the bride and groom and their exact birth places and residences. Sadly, most couples in Cook County did not fill out this application. Our ancestors got the fast track, so to speak, of getting married and only had to fill out a form nearly identical to that of the marriage license. The only new piece of information that could be gained from a Cook County marriage application is the groom's address, which often is written on the top of the application.

These documents can only be found in the Cook County clerk's office. Some couples did fill out the more detailed application, especially in South Chicago, but the majority did not. I recommend spending $15 for the application only for tricky situations but not for every couple in your family tree.

C. Death Certificates

There are five main types of death certificates used in Cook County genealogy research. Death certificates are fairly easy to find, because some form of proof of death was needed for a burial permit. A death certificate was the easiest way to do just that. Sadly, infants and children are easily found in civil death records, but no trace of them may be found in civil birth records. That was just the nature of record keeping back then.

The record used from 1871 until 1895 is the first type of death certificate. These records generally are written in sloppy cursive handwriting with little regard for the spelling of the person's name. LDS has published its 1878–1922 Cook County death certificate collection on www.familysearch.org, so the original images of these death records are freely accessible to the general public.

The state of Illinois has two databases of death records from Cook County on its Cyberdrive website:

http://www.cyberdriveillinois.com/departments/archives/databases.html

Both sites have the same information, but the key difference is that the LDS site has the images to back up the information whereas Illinois only gives the information transcribed by volunteers. I recommend beginning to search for death certificates on the LDS website. If the record cannot be found on the LDS website, then search the Illinois website, because a different transcriber recorded the names on that site.

The information found on these early death certificates is decent but not the best. On an early death certificate, the name of the decedent, gender, date of death, age at death, occupation, place of burial, address of death, duration of disease that led to death, and the name of the undertaker are listed. Generally, the name of the cemetery will be given as "Polish Cemetery," "Bohemian Polish Cemetery," or "Bohemian Cemetery." However, most of the time, these names all signified St. Adalbert Cemetery in Niles, not Bohemian National Cemetery. These were just a nicknames used then to refer to St. Adalbert.

The next form type used is similar to these early death certificates. It had basically the same information on it. The key difference between these death certificates is that from 1896 until 1910, there was a box at the bottom of the death certificate with space to write the cause(s) of death and then how long each cause plagued the person also could be written in the box next to the cause. Also, space to record information about the doctor who attended to the person before their death was added. A variant of this form was the hospital death certificate if the person died in a hospital. All the information is the same;

the only thing added was the name of the hospital where the person died along with the deceased's prior residence. The handwriting on these forms tends to be a lot neater than the earlier records.

After 1910, death certificates became much more detailed and organized. From 1910 until 1916, a new death certificate form with a new organizational scheme was introduced. It is mostly the same information, just with a cleaner and neater organization. New information added to these death certificates included the full names of the decedent's father and mother; how long the person had been in the country, state, and city; and the hour of burial. There was also space added that allowed the listing of two different occupations and the duration that the deceased worked at each occupation. All this information sounds like genealogical gold, but the problem is that often this information was not filled out or was just hastily filled out. Sometimes the parents' names are given but not always. It all comes down to luck whether information about that particular person was conveyed by his or her surviving family to the clerk filling out the death certificate.

Although there are some slight variations between the years, I consider all 1916–1947 death certificates as modern death certificates. Their schema is still used today with only slight modifications; otherwise the content is all the same. They are rich and detailed and contain all kinds of excellent information about the deceased's life.

On these modern death certificates, a genealogist can expect to find a number of important pieces of information. These include

- the deceased's full name
- home address
- place of death (if different than home address)
- how long a resident in Chicago
- how long a resident in the United States
- gender
- marital status
- name of spouse if married or widowed
- date of birth
- age
- birthplace
- occupational trade and job title within that trade
- name of employer
- full name of parents along with the birthplaces of parents
- name and address of the informant who gave all of this information
- whether the person has ever been in the military
- date of death and detailed information about cause of death and any secondary symptoms that contributed to that death
- name of coroner who issued death certificate
- place of burial, date of burial, and the name of the undertaker.

Some information was added or modified as the years passed. Starting in the late 1930s, the deceased's social security number, if available, began to be recorded on death certificates. Also, the medical information section relating to death was altered a bit over the years.

Images of these death certificates are available for free on www.familysearch.org for Cook County until 1922. After that, LDS has a transcribed database with information from all death certificates in Illinois between 1916 and 1947 but without images. Ancestry also has a transcribed database of information from this records collection. While the transcriptions are good and can help verify who is who in the search for death certificates, a transcription is no replacement for an original record.

Microfilm images of original death certificates for Cook County from 1916 until 1947 are located in the State Archives in Springfield, Illinois. Simply viewing these images on microfilm is free, but printouts cost fifty cents each. It is worth a trip to Springfield to get copies of these death certificates, because they are rich in information. Information about decedents between the years of 1948 and 1950 can be found on the Cyberdrive website's database, but the actual certificates are not available for viewing via microfilm in Springfield.

Modern death certificates, those kept after 1950, have the same information on them as the previous kind of death certificates. Sometimes the boxes are in different places, some were typed on a typewriter, but they are pretty much the same. Copies of these can only be purchased from the Cook County Clerk using its website or by visiting the Cook County Complex at the Daily Center in downtown Chicago.

Death certificates are a must for all genealogists. Knowing when your ancestors died is just as important as knowing when they were born or got married. A lot of great information about the people of the past can be found on their death certificates.

Death certificates are excellent resources for genealogists. Use the information found in census records to find these death certificates. Also, the obituary index on the PGSA website can help you find death information. Flip to Chapter Six for more information about how to find other records that can help locate the death certificate for a particular ancestor.

Section 2: Church

The years of mass emigration from Poland were also years of booming industry, rapid expansion, and high optimism for the city of Chicago. The Stockyards, steel works, and other industries were magnets drawing in Poles to provide the massive amounts of labor needed in these industries. The city was growing physically, economically, and politically so that the city of 1880 bore little resemblance to the city of 1930.

One institution that did bear a resemblance between 1880 and 1930 was the Catholic Church of Chicago. Pre-partition Poland was known throughout Europe as a great haven of religious tolerance in a sea of intolerance and discrimination. Therefore, there was a wide variety of religions in Poland, ranging from the Greek Uniate Church to Lutheranism to Calvinism. Generally speaking, from the 1700s onward, Protestantism was confined to the German immigrants who settled in Poland along with some upper-class Poles who intermarried with these Germans.

Aside from the large Jewish population, the vast majority of ethnic Poles were Catholics. More importantly for this book, the vast majority of Poles who immigrated to Chicago were Catholics. Therefore, I will cover the Catholic Church records of Chicago. There were no "Polish" Lutheran churches, only German Lutheran churches, so if your ancestors were Polish Lutherans, then research Germans in Cook County to find their parish records.

Catholic Church records in Cook County were kept in Latin throughout the course of the nineteenth century and most were kept in Latin in the twentieth century. St. Stanislaus Kostka Church is one exception that used the Polish language in many of its records. Some parishes also used Polish when they created informal death records. No Polish parishes used English as an official record-keeping language until after World War I and some not until after the Vatican II Catholic Church reforms of the 1960s.

Do not be intimidated by church records in Latin. A lot of English is derived from the dialect of French spoken by the Norman conquerors of England, which in turn was derived from Latin. Therefore, many common words in English are structurally similar to their counterparts in Latin. The three types of Latin records found are the *liber baptizorum* (baptism book), *liber copulatorum* (marriage book), and *liber sepultarum* or mortuorum (death book). Knowledge of Spanish or French will make learning Latin easier because they are Romance languages, descended from the mother tongue of Latin.

After mastering some basic Latin vocabulary such as *et* (and), *nomen* (name), and *cognomen* (surname), deciphering the Latin records of your ancestors will be no problem. Figuring out what a Latin record says is not that difficult, because church records were kept in a standard format for births, marriages, deaths, etc. Once one baptism record has been deciphered, then virtually every other one will come easily.

Use the Internet to look up what unknown words mean. LDS has an excellent Latin word list to use for genealogical purposes: https://wiki.familysearch.org/en/Latin_Genealogical_Word_List

There are two ways to access the records of the Catholic Churches of Chicago. The traditional way is to visit a family history library set up by the Church of Latter Day Saints (LDS). If you live in the Chicagoland area, visit the libraries in Naperville or Waukegan, because both locations have large collections of Polish Catholic Church records. However, if you do not live in the Chicagoland area, then you can access all of the Catholic Church records of Chicago online on the LDS website. There is currently an indexing project that seeks to index all of the Catholic Church records of Chicago. When completed, it will make finding church records vastly easier than before.

Today, ethnicity is not that important when it comes to which Catholic Church to attend. However, in the late 1800s and early 1900s, church attendance was based upon ethnicity. Each nationality in Chicago had its own separate churches. Mixing among nationalities became more and more common as the years wore on, but early on, people stuck within their own nationalities and churches. The Polish of Chicago tended to be the models of this rule. I have found that Polish people married people of other nationalities a lot less than other nationalities did.

The key difference between finding vital records issued by the county versus vital records from churches is that you need to know which church your ancestors attended as opposed to the county, which has everyone in its database.

How Do I Determine Which Church My Ancestors Attended?

There were more than twenty specifically Polish Catholic churches in the Chicago area in the first half of the 1900s. The easiest way to find the correct church of ancestry is to use the Polish Genealogical Society of America (PGSA) website: www.pgsa.org. The PGSA has a marriage index of all marriages in Polish parishes from the beginning of these churches until 1915. It also has a limited birth index of certain parishes in Cook County and elsewhere. I recommend searching for your ancestors first in the marriage database, and then in the birth index to find your ancestors' parish.

Finding the church on the PGSA website is the easiest way to do this. If they are not found, then they must have been married in Poland or elsewhere. A handy tool to find families not on the PGSA website is to use Rootsweb: http://www.rootsweb.ancestry.com/~itappcnc/pipcnchicagochurches.htm

This page lists all Catholic churches of Chicago along with their founding year and main nationality served. This is a great guide for finding the Polish parishes in Chicago. The best functionality is the tool used to locate a parish based upon the geographic coordinates of your ancestors' residences; it provides the parishes located near those coordinates. This allows you to determine which churches are close to where your ancestors lived.

Keep in mind that people generally did not travel very far in the past, especially in the late 1800s, so they would have attended a church close to their home, most likely within walking distance. If they lived on the South Side, then they would have attended a South Side church, not a North Side church. Also, people wanted to stick with others of their nationality, so they would have gone to the Polish parish even if the Irish or Italian church was closer to their home. Finding the correct parish will be trial and error, but there are a finite number of parishes, so you will eventually find the right one. Next, see what years are covered on microfilm and plan accordingly.

The first officially Polish parish in Chicago was St. Stanislaus Kostka, which opened in 1867 on the North Side of Chicago. The first Polish parish on the South Side was St. Adalbert Church, which opened in 1874. Before then, Poles attended the German or Bohemian Catholic churches in Chicago.

Before St. Adalbert opened, my ancestors attended St. John Nepomucene Bohemian Church, which opened in 1871, and then St. Wenceslaus Bohemian Church before that. For people of South Side ancestry, review the records of these parishes to see if your ancestors were listed as godparents or witnesses.

Catholic Church records are the main source of genealogical information in Poland. In the United States, these records are consistent but not incredibly detailed. More information generally can be found on secular records, especially for South Side Chicago Poles.

A. Baptisms

Baptism records of the Catholic Churches of Cook County are generally the most reliable records that can be found. When I say reliable, I mean that the information found on them is fairly uniform from parish to parish. In fact, most parishes used the same pre-printed sheets to fill in the information about the child being baptized.

All baptism records include the child's name, date of baptism, father's full name, mother's first and maiden, and the child's godparents' names. Early records tend to be scrawled in big lists whereas later baptism records were recorded in neat boxes on pre-printed sheets. Usually the date of birth was given.

Sometimes the priest would also record information in the margin about that child's eventual marriage or death, but this is uncommon. There is not much difference between baptism records on the North Side or the South Side.

B. First Communions/Confirmations

Of the church records found in Cook County, communion records have the least amount of information and are the least common to find. These records are just lists of children who completed their First Communion at that parish.

Confirmation records have the child's name along with the name that he or she chose at Confirmation. No hard genealogical facts are in these records aside from confirmation that this was indeed the parish your ancestors attended. They are nice records nonetheless. They help provide depth to your ancestors aside from when they were born or married, for example. These records are worth a look, but don't spend too much time on them.

C. Marriages

Marriage records clearly illustrate the disparity in record keeping between the North Side and South Side Catholic parishes. Marriage records on the South Side were short and to the point versus records from the North Side, which are wonderful sources of information and can help trace your family back to its ancestral village in Poland.

The three big parishes on the South Side were Sts. Peter and Paul, St. Adalbert, and St. Mary of Perpetual Help. South Side church marriage records from the late 1800s until the end of the 1900s did not have much information in them. The marriage records from these parishes only listed the date of marriage, bride and groom's full names, and two witnesses to the marriage. Sometimes the parents of the bride and groom would be listed. It wasn't until the 1910s that parents began being listed on all marriage records.

When a marriage record asked where a person lived, only "Chicago" would be listed or a Chicago neighborhood, such as "Bridgeport." Later marriage records would ask for a place of birth, but only "Illinois" or "Poland" would be listed. In short, these marriage records are decent but do not contain nearly as much information compared with the marriage records of the North Side.

The main churches on the North Side were St. Stanislaus Kostka, Holy Trinity, and St. John Cantius—the big three churches of North Side Chicago Polonia. Of these, St. Stanislaus Kostka was the oldest and largest. It also has the best records of any parish in the Chicagoland area, in my opinion.

Marriage records from St. Stanislaus Kostka are beautiful. They always depict the date of marriage, the full name of the bride and groom, the full name of their parents, and information about the witnesses. Marriage records from the 1880s onward even included each person's true place of birth, down to the village and county in Poland. This information led me across the ocean to my ancestral village for one specific family line. It was fantastic. These marriage records also list the respective addresses of the groom and bride, the dates of the marriage banns (proclamation of the intention of a couple to marry that is contained within the church books), and the signatures of the witnesses to the wedding.

Not all North Side parishes have this level of information, but they generally do have most of this, even the specific place of birth. In general, do not expect too much from South Side marriage records.

D. Deaths/Funerals

If your ancestor died in Poland in the 1880s, the priest would have written a detailed death record, probably listing the deceased's parents, cause of death, living relatives, and other information about him or her. In Chicago at this time, there is virtually nothing.

South Side parishes did not even begin keeping death records until the mid-1880s. Even then, they were not true death records; they were funeral records. The only death records that South Side churches kept in the late 1800s were funeral registries recording who had a funeral at that church and how much it cost. The typical child's funeral cost fifty cents whereas an adult's cost between four and five dollars. These registries recorded the name of the deceased, approximately how old he or she was, and how much the funeral cost.

Secular death certificates from this time tell a lot more about the person. Relying on church death records is not a wise strategy simply because it is impossible to verifying the person. Don't be fooled by someone the same age as your relative; it has happened to me before. Use other sources to verify that this person truly was your ancestor.

North Side parishes were not much better, but their records were more standard. They began keeping death records (mostly just funeral registries) in the 1870s in the same manner as South Side parishes. However, they soon evolved into proper death records that recorded the name of the person, date of death, age at death, cause of death, parents or spouse of the deceased, and maybe some other information. They still are not perfect, but they are better than South Side death records.

Conclusion

Sifting through the millions of records generated by the Catholic church in Chicago may seem like a daunting task. However, do not fear. LDS has published all of the church books of Chicago's Catholic parishes before 1915 on its FamilySearch.org website, so these can be browsed at your leisure. It has begun an indexing project of all of the information found in them. Once this massive index is done, then finding information in the church books will be much, much easier.

Hopefully between government vital records and church vital records, some vital information can be found about your ancestors. If after all that searching, nothing still comes up, then your ancestors must have lived elsewhere. Polish Catholics used the church system as well as the government for their vital record keeping. I can't find half of the birth certificates for my ancestors, but I have found all but one baptism record. This is because reporting births costs money and was not really necessary then. Unless your ancestor was born in a hospital or had a doctor attending the birth, perhaps no one actually recorded the birth.

Church records in America are good for helping solidify facts, such as exact birth dates, about individual people. They can be used to back up or refute information found in census records. One major advantage to these records is that they were recorded by Polish-speaking priests. Therefore, the spelling of your ancestors' names should have only minor variances, if any. There are few ridiculous name spellings as with census records or other secular records. This is especially a plus in the late 1800s, when there weren't many other types of records. Sometimes vital records can lead back to a village of origin. That is not always the case, so it is necessary to search for other types of records, such as immigration, emigration, and naturalization records.

CHAPTER FOUR: NATURALIZATION RECORDS

Soundex and Database Searching

Naturalization documents in the Chicagoland area are somewhat useful to Polish–American researchers, but it depends when the ancestor in question got naturalized. The naturalization laws of the United States have been in upheaval in the past few decades, but luckily for genealogists, your ancestor's naturalization documents will be in one of four categories.

The general rule of thumb is that the more recent the person was naturalized, the more information will be found on his or her naturalization document. Older naturalization documents still have value; they just are not the magical keys to the family history they could have been if recorded a few decades later.

The traditional way to obtain a naturalization document is to look it up in the soundex index created by the government as part of the Works Progress Administration's effort to make jobs for people in the 1930s. A soundex is a special index in which workers keyed information from Cook County naturalization documents and then organized them based on the letters in a person's surname. Search a soundex by looking at certain letters in a person's surname and then finding their corresponding numbers in the soundex chart.

To search a soundex, take the first letter of the person's surname, set it aside, and then write out the other consonants in that surname. After writing out the consonants, find their corresponding numbers on the chart. Now, take that first letter and the first three numbers and string them together. You should now have a code with a consonant at the beginning and then three numbers at the end (use zeros if your surname has less than four consonants). This is the soundex system used by the National Archives:

Letter – Corresponding Number
B F P V – 1
C G J K Q S X Z – 2
D T – 3
L – 4
M N – 5
R – 6

Vowels do not get letters and neither do H, W, or Y.

More information about this method of records organization and about the naturalization soundex in particular can be found in this NARA publication: http://www.archives.gov/research/microfilm/m1285.pdf

To find a surname in the soundex chart, simply look at the consonants in a person's surname and then generate a corresponding number. For example, an ancestor who has continually eluded my search for his naturalization documents is my great-grandfather John Bara. I have searched for him repeatedly in the soundex index by looking at his surname. The first letter is B, so I set that aside, then I write out the only consonant he had, R. R corresponds to 6. The soundex code I generated was B600. I will then look in the B600 files for his naturalization document. Another example is Barczynski. B – R – C – Z – N – K. This soundex code would be B622. This was a nifty way of searching for surnames that have multiple spellings or were so foreign that the English-speaking clerks had difficulty transcribing them.

Before the advent of the home computer, the soundex system for naturalizations was wonderful. The information needed to be organized somehow, and the soundex made sense for immigrants whose surnames probably would be misspelled in the official documents. The soundex does not record vowels, the most easily messed-up part of a person's surname, so in that respect, the soundex is useful.

The volunteers at the World Archives Project at Ancestry.com have completed keying the information from the soundex index, so now a person need only type in a name on their website and the results will immediately pop up. I keyed more 3,000 naturalization cards and was very pleased with the results.

Because volunteers contributed to the World Archives Project, the index is free for to the public, but a subscription is needed to view the images. No subscription? No problem. Simply visit www.familysearch.org, go to the Illinois collections, and see the published free naturalization soundex image cards. You can browse those cards using the soundex method of searching. However, I recommend searching for the surname on Ancestry and scrolling through the results first. Looking after card after card after card in the soundex index is rather tedious. LDS currently has a project to key this information, which will also be free to search.

Each soundex card will have the person's first and last names, notation for the record (i.e., the court where the person was naturalized), and some kind of docket or book number. Almost all cards have a country of origin and the date of naturalization. Some cards have the address, the date of entry to the United States, the port of entry, and the names of witnesses to the naturalization and possibly their respective addresses. Finally, some cards have unusual tidbits detailing information such as whether the person expatriated him or herself by moving back to the old country. The type of information found on the card depends on which time period your ancestor was naturalized.

Soundex cards have great initial information, but it is imperative to find the original naturalization record to gain the greatest amount of value from it. All extant records have been indexed in this soundex index. Therefore, the soundex card will tell what type of record will be found for that particular person, but I am getting ahead of myself. Without that card, finding the original naturalization document is difficult. It can be done but not easily.

Naturalization Process

There are two steps to the naturalization process during the period that is of interest to most Polish–American genealogists (1870s-1940s). First, an immigrant would file the declaration of intent. This was considered the "first papers" of naturalization, and if an immigrant had already filed these by the time the census came around, then "PA" would be written in his or her record which basically means the person's naturalization status was pending. After the declaration of intent, the final papers would declare that person to be a citizen.

Something to keep in mind is that only men could become naturalized citizens of the United States before the 1920s. A woman's citizenship status was based on her husband's. If he was an alien, she was, too. In fact, many natural-born women in the United States had to file for citizenship in the 1930s and 1940s, because they married foreign-born men and, in so doing, lost their U.S. citizenship. If her husband naturalized, a woman could become a full-fledged U.S. citizen.

If your ancestor came before the Ellis Island era, then she probably did not file her own naturalization documents. If she came during or after the era, she probably did. It is worth a shot to check all of your female ancestors, but if their husbands filed before the 1920s, the odds that they did their own naturalization process are slim to none.

1. Early Naturalizations: 1871-1906

Naturalizations have been done in Chicago since the 1830s, but a little thing called the Great Chicago Fire destroyed all naturalization documents completed before 1871. So as with vital records, 1871 is the starting date for naturalization records in Chicago. Some Poles were naturalized before 1871, but unfortunately, those documents are now gone.

Naturalization documents completed before 1906 have little information. The typical information is the person's name, date of naturalization, court of naturalization, and country of origin. The country will most likely be that of the partitioning power: Germany, Russia, or Austria. It will have something such as Germany–Poland or Russia–Polish, but when sifting through soundex cards, do not get discouraged if "Poland" is not written on the card because it probably will not be.

The average naturalization document is in a ledger book and thus is on oversized, legal-sized paper. It is a standard, typed form with a few spots for information to be written in. It contains the first and last name, the country of origin, and the date of naturalization. It may contain your ancestor's signature and address and the signature and address of a witness. People who wished to be naturalized needed character witnesses to prove to the court that they were good and upstanding members of the community. Ironically, out of all my ancestors, only one falls in this "normal" category.

"Court Order Only" cards are frustrating to researchers. A soundex card with those three infamous words typed across one of the lines means that your ancestor's naturalization document no longer exists. The actual record is lost, most likely gone forever. This type of naturalization document is a standard, typed form that only contains your ancestor's name scrawled across it. That is all. I still get copies of those court orders, but they are indeed disappointing to behold.

If the person was a minor when coming to the United States, he or she would have followed a separate procedure for becoming a citizen. Minors did not have to file declarations of intent; they needed only to come in with a witness and declare their citizenship. Minors' naturalization documents are actually relatively detailed. Usually, the name, country of origin, signature, and possibly an address can be found on a minor's naturalization.

How many years that minor had been in the country may have been recorded as well, which is crucial to know for genealogy. I have found that years of immigration on census records tend to be conservative estimates such as "20 years" or "25 years" in

America rather than exact numbers. However, the minors' naturalizations petitions often give an exact year, which makes the search for ship records much easier. That is the most valuable piece of information found on minors' naturalization documents. Use this information to search ship records for your ancestor's passenger manifest entry.

These early naturalizations are more sparse in information when compared with later naturalizations, but they are still of great value because they document what was left behind in the past. Their symbolic value is enormous; that little piece of paper was a ticket to a better life in America. It symbolized our ancestors' hopes and dreams of rising up and bettering themselves in this strange, new country. Seeking original copies of these naturalization documents is still good to do, because they are part of the relatively small paper trail that our ancestors left more than one hundred years ago.

2. Middle Naturalizations: 1907-1920s

The years 1904 to 1906 were a transition period for naturalization law, and the documents encountered in that gap have elements of the old naturalizations and the middle naturalization documents. They have the same information as before, but they might include the applicant's address and date of entry to the United States. Then in 1906, everything changed.

The U.S. government tightened regulations with regard to naturalizations and immigration, which is reflected in the amount of information required to naturalize a person. Naturalization documents from this era are more detailed and consequently cover more sheets of paper. An effort is being made by the Cook County Clerk's office to index declarations of intent for this period, and their preliminary results are searchable at http://www.cookcountyclerkofcourt.org/NR/.

In addition to the information listed on previous records, declarations of intent from this era added a description of the person, a town of origin, and immigration information including the port of origin, ship's name, and date of arrival. Records from this era generally are reliable and have good information. Sometimes the exact immigration information is not given, but there should be enough information to help point in the right direction.

The certificate of naturalization document has even better information—information about the applicant's family. Much of the same information from the declaration of intent is found in the certificate, but the additional information is that the applicant's children and their birthdays will be listed. The applicant's spouse will be listed too. This familial information is wonderful to have. It helps add to the information found in civil and church vital records.

These records will be mostly of men, but women begin to show up in the 1920s, after they got the right to vote.

3. Recent Naturalizations: 1920s-1940s

As time wore on, naturalizations became more complicated and time consuming. Later naturalization records continue to build on the information found in the records of previous eras. More detailed information about where the applicant was born along with the vital information of their spouse and children are included. The best part about later naturalization records is that they will include a photograph of the applicant. The only early photograph I have of my great grandfather is the tiny photo on his declaration of intent to become a citizen filed in 1935.

How Can I Obtain a Copy of the Original Records?

Obtain a copy of the original records in downtown Chicago at the Archives of the Cook County Court using that naturalization soundex card. All relevant information including hours and procedures for research is found at their website: http://www.cookcountyclerkofcourt.org/?RecArchivePage=6000&section=RecArchivePage

I do not recommend visiting the court without the soundex card. It is possible to search for your ancestor in indexes of declarations of intent that have been microfilmed by LDS, but this method is not the best. The archive employees have been trained to read soundex cards, but they get uncomfortable when presented with something else.

Order copies of these records from home using the mail-in form or hire a professional to get copies for you. However, I seriously advise going in person. Take a look at the actual records; they will actually bring them out to examine before they photocopy them. They will also find other records at the archives including divorce, probate, and other court documents (see Chapter Seven).

An alternate route to obtaining naturalization documents is to contact the U.S. Citizenship and Immigration Services department: http://www.uscis.gov/portal/site/uscis

They have copies of post-1906 naturalization documents from across the country. This is a good route to take if the location of naturalization for your ancestor is unknown or could be in different counties. However, going to the Cook County archives is the best bet for Chicago ancestry.

Conclusion

Immigration law has its tricks and loopholes like many parts of the legal system, and it would take a volume of this size to go through every "what if" scenario. My best advice is to think about your ancestor's life and determine why your ancestor would have become a citizen, if he or she even did. I have found that early Polish immigrants to Chicago often were not naturalized. Peter Mroz came to Chicago in 1869, and I have yet to find a naturalization document for him. His cousin Frank Mroz came some time in the late 1860s, but he never was naturalized. However, I did find naturalization documents for Peter's children; his sons were naturalized so they could vote in elections.

Census records can provide clues for naturalization but are not the end-all, be-all solution. Starting with the 1900 census, census takers asked people whether they were naturalized citizens. Sometimes the census gave a year of naturalization; sometimes it did not. Like all census data, this information needs to be taken with a grain of salt. It can help to point in the right direction, but it is not the final solution.

Sometimes people filed their declarations of intent but did not follow through to become citizens. If this happened, they will not have a soundex card attached to their record, because soundex cards were only issued to people who filed their final papers and officially became citizens. Determining whether this was what a person did can be tricky.

Maybe their declaration of intent will be in the partial database that the Cook County Clerk is working on. However, the most likely strategy is to sift through court indexes. LDS has microfilmed some declaration-of-intent indexes for Chicago courts. There are also some indexes at the court's archives.

If your ancestor was an Ellis Island immigrant, he or she most likely did become a citizen. Just keep searching. My elusive ancestor is John Bara, my great grandfather. All his census documents said he was a naturalized citizen. Sadly, I have no proof. That's part of the fun of genealogy—determining how to triumph over all sorts of setbacks.

CHAPTER FIVE: U.S. MILITARY RECORDS

Early Military Service

Military records are heralded as tremendous instruments of genealogical information, and that is no exception to the Poles of Chicago. It is now time for you to find those patriotic ancestors who nobly served in America's armed forces. Well, this section would be a lot longer and more detailed if I had picked an ethnicity such as German or Scottish, which have been well represented in the United States since before the Revolution.

Of course there was Pulaski and Kosciuszko in the American Revolution along with a few other Poles who fought in America's early wars. However, the odds of finding a Polish military ancestor would be like finding the ancestor who left a Swiss bank account filled with millions of dollars worth of gold ingots for the person who can prove direct descent from them. Unless you are descended from a Polish pioneer such as Anthony Sadowski, the odds of finding a Polish ancestor who fought in the American Revolution or War of 1812 would be astronomical.

Thousands of Poles served in the Civil War, mostly for the Union but some did fight for the Confederacy, most notably those from the early Panna Maria settlement and other areas of Texas. A famous Pole who served was General Wlodzimierz (Vladimir) Krzyzanowski who was the head of the "Polish Regiment" in the Union forces and fought at the Battle of Gettysburg. My in-law relative Peter Kiolbassa was a famous Chicagoan who served first for the Confederacy but was captured and joined the Union forces and rose to the rank of cavalry captain.

Those who fought in the Civil War were mainly early immigrants who had been here since the mid-1850s. The best place to search for Civil War ancestors is in one of the many indexes available online, either on Ancestry, Fold3, or most recently the LDS site. The LDS index is, as always, free, but Ancestry and Fold3 have more detailed information, so be sure to use one of those sites if LDS has some information about him. The odds of finding a Polish ancestor in the Civil War are slim, but it is definitely possible.

Based on the research I have done, few Polish immigrants actively joined the armed forces. Please don't send me nasty letters telling about your patriotic ancestors who joined the army the minute they got off the boat. I said at the beginning that absolute statements are meaningless in genealogy.

The reality was that conscription was in full force when the partitioning powers chopped up Poland, and many young men were forced into service in all three of the partitioning areas. It is much more likely that your ancestor served in the Prussian army than the American army. European military service is covered in Chapter Twelve.

In America, many Polish immigrants wanted a fresh start and a way to make a living with their industrial and urban jobs and not be shipped from army base to army base. I have found that Polish emigrants joined the American armed forces in low numbers, but their children and grandchildren joined in the same numbers, proportionally speaking, as other American groups.

My example of this is my gg-grandfather Valentine Stefaniak. He served in the Prussian military before immigrating to America in 1872. He did not join the American army, but his son, John Stefaniak, joined the U.S. Marine Corps in 1906 and served for four years under the name John Stefanak. Later immigrant ancestors of mine joined the military as well, especially during World War II.

The best way to find a Polish military ancestor between the Civil War and World War I is to use a pre-existing index. Ancestry has an excellent index for the U.S. Marine Corps before World War II, which I used to find my ancestor. It also has a database for the U.S. Army before World War I that details enlistments to the U.S. army during that period.

LDS has images of army enlistments from 1790 to 1914, and its army of volunteer indexers is working on a searchable database for these records. This will be an excellent index that will prove to be invaluable to all Americans, including those of Polish descent. Ancestry has this same information on its website, so you can view it there for fee. Or you could go to www.familysearch.org/indexing and become a part of this indexing effort.

The U.S. Navy is trickier because it had fewer members than the army. I helped key the Naval Enlistment project, which has been published on the LDS site for the years 1855 to 1891. It probably won't help many Polish researchers, but hopefully some can find relatives in it.

A word of warning is that the navy was the loneliest branch of the armed forces, so to speak. It was mostly young, single men choosing the life of the sea along with some grizzled maritime veterans. It would be rare to find a man with a wife and children in Illinois enlisting in the navy.

The Illinois Cyberdrive website also has some military databases that have information from this time:
http://www.cyberdriveillinois.com/departments/archives/databases.html

If those don't yield anything, then your ancestor probably did not serve in the American armed forces. However, if you are positive that your ancestor did serve, write the U.S. National Personnel Records Center (NPRC) in St. Louis to have them do a search for his records: http://www.archives.gov/st-louis/

This center holds the military records for a wide variety of years and services and will be the starting point for military research. Fill out the SF-180 for most veterans and then wait up to eight months for a response. The website explains the details, because depending on the branch and estimated years of service, a certain form is needed and will be sent to a particular address, either in St. Louis or Washington D.C.

That was the tricky part. Pre-World War I military research is difficult. Post-World War I research is easier but will probably yield less information. No, that was not a typo. A great fire ripped through the St. Louis records center in the 1970s and destroyed many army records from World War I and later along with the records of other branches. Therefore, finding an ancestor's military documents from 1914 onward will be a great roll of the dice. My grandmother's brother, Henry Smith, had his service record survive, but there are singe marks on the edges. Others, such as my cousin Henry Jozwiak, will have no surviving documentation, and NPRC will merely say that such a person did serve, but no documents exist to provide further information.

The staff at the St. Louis NPRC is helpful, and its employees do their best to locate your ancestors' files. Be patient because they get thousands of requests. Sometimes the search will take a few weeks. The longest search I've experienced was approximately eight months. Be as detailed as possible with this paperwork and hope for the best.

How Do I Know If an Ancestor Served in the Military in World War I and Beyond?

1. Draft Cards

World War I

The World War I draft card index is an excellent resource for all men of military age in the United States regardless of whether they were citizens. There were three different calls for the draft depending on when the person was born. Men born between 1877 and 1900 had to fill out the card at some point. I got lucky; my gg-grandmother's brother was born in 1874 and still filled out a draft card. He probably didn't want to take any chances and figured it was better to be safe than sorry because draft evasion was a serious crime.

The first and second draft calls were for men who were actually expected to serve—those born between 1886 and 1896 and 1896 and 1897, respectively. The third call for the draft extended the time span for the birth date of registration to 1877 to 1900. On the cards for the older men, the man's name, address, employer, date of birth, nearest relative, physical description, and other miscellaneous information will be found. They also had to sign their cards. A personal signature is definitely a nice touch; too bad photos weren't taken as well!

The draft cards from the first and second call ask for mostly the same information but also ask for previous military experience as well as reasons for exemption from the draft.

The beauty of this index is that it captured many Polish immigrants in a nice card that provides a physical description and many other clues that will lead to more records. Searching for World War II draft cards is an absolute necessity in Polish–American genealogy.

If there is no draft card for an ancestor, then that might mean that he already signed up and fought in the war, as was the case for my great grandfather. Then again, it may be that Ancestry never filmed your ancestor's card, as was the case for my great grandfather John Kruszka and his brother Lawrence Kruszka. Do some serious sleuthing, because the coverage for the World War I draft card index was virtually the entire male population of that age, so a card should exist for your ancestor. It could also mean that he did not live in the United States in 1917 or 1918.

World War II

The same is true of the World War II draft card index. The most genealogically significant collection is the so-called "old man's" draft for World War II. Just like in World War I, the U.S. government conducted four different draft registrations with the fourth and final one being for the oldest men in the U.S. population—those born after 1877 and were not in the military already. So the coverage for the U.S. population is just as great for this draft. The easiest cards to find are from the fourth draft, because they are available for Illinois online on Ancestry with a searchable database with images or on LDS where the browsable images have been posted.

The earlier drafts were done for those who were actually going to be conscripted into service—those aged eighteen to mid-twenties. Copies of records from the previous three drafts are stored in the National Archives and Records Administration (NARA) office on Pulaski Road in Chicago where the actual cards are housed because none of those are online for Illinois. This website has all details: http://www.archives.gov/great-lakes/

The fourth draft will probably be the most helpful for genealogists, but it is nice to get records from our parents and grandparents too, so it is worth a trip to NARA. All research done on World War II and afterward needs to be done in person at NARA. Selective service cards are housed there for the later 1940s and 1950s for more recent ancestors. None of that is available online because of privacy laws.

As with World War II, if there is no draft card for a man of military age, then he probably already signed up with the armed services. Millions of Americans were involved in this war by directly fighting, nursing the wounded, building planes, etc. Patriotism was high in the country, and the Poles were no exception to this.

2. Online Indices

There is a plethora of twentieth-century military records available on Ancestry. It is definitely worth a subscription to Ancestry just to explore them. Ancestry has brought millions of records online from this period and will definitely help to locate your military ancestors. One beautiful collection that Ancestry released in 2011 was the BIRLS military death index. This database has information about any serviceman or woman who received a benefit of some kind from the government (education via the GI bill, a pension, etc) and who is deceased today. This database will contain that person's name, dates of service, birthday, and maybe some more information about him or her. This covers some people from WWI and then all veterans from WWII onwards who are deceased today, so it is an excellent way to find information about military ancestors and relatives whose records were destroyed in the St. Louis fire.

NARA also has an online database of World War II enlistments: http://aad.archives.gov/aad/series-description.jsp?s=3360. This database is by no means complete, but it is a valuable resource. The most important piece of information found in it will be the service number of a particular veteran. This is a crucial piece of information to give to the NPRC in St. Louis. Without the veteran's service number, then the search for a service record will take much longer and may not yield good results. A service number guarantees that the researchers in St. Louis will look in the right places for information about your ancestor's service.

Fold3, formerly known as www.footnote.com has actually rebranded itself as a military research website. Its specialty is American military research, so it is definitely worth a subscription in order to find your military ancestors.

LDS also have military resources available. A search of the Chicago Tribune's Historical Archives may also yield some information in the form of news articles about enlistments, discharges, and deaths in the military. Public libraries in the Chicagoland area should have a subscription to this database; talk to the reference librarian at a local public library to find out the details.

I recommend searching on Ancestry first and then try writing to the NPRC in St. Louis to determine exactly what your ancestor did. Also, refer to the notes from your original investigations into family history (see Chapter One). If an ancestor served in World War II, then a relative probably would have told you, because this was a very recent war. Military records can be genealogical goldmines and can prove your family's patriotism. They are some of my favorites to read because they give a sense of what kind of a person this ancestor was.

Military records probably will not help to research female ancestors because of the small number of women serving in the armed forces from 1860 to 1945. However, widows' pension collections have many details. If your ancestor served in the armed forces between the Civil War and World War II, his widow may have applied for a pension after he died. He also could have applied for a pension if he was injured in the war, or if it caused some other ill effects in his life. Those records are found on Ancestry, Fold3, and on LDS as well. It's a long shot for Polish genealogists, but they are there for those lucky few.

Another resource that should be mentioned is Haller's Army. The PGSA has compiled a wonderful index of service records for the men who served in this particular regiment during World War I. The Great War was seen as the opportunity for the Poles to rise up against the partitioning powers and regain their freedom, so many Poles from America wanted to do their part to fight for Poland. They formed a company known as Haller's Army for this express purpose. Good information about the people who served in it can be found in the records held by the PGSA; the online index with this information is at http://www.pgsa.org/haller.php.

The Poles have proven their worth time and time again in the heat of battle, and the American military was no exception. The fees for the service records of your ancestors can get pricey, especially if they served in the Marine Corps or Navy before World War I, but those records are worth every penny. They provide great insight into our ancestors' lives in a way that no other records can. Do not hesitate to purchase a copy of a service record.

CHAPTER SIX: CEMETERIES, BURIALS, FUNERALS, AND RELATED DEATH RECORDS

A. Newspaper Obituaries

Dziennik Chicagoski

The easiest place to look for a Pole's death record in Chicago is in the Dziennik Chicagoski database on the PGSA's website. The PGSA has indexed the obituaries and death entries for the entire run of one of Chicago's largest and most-read Polish newspapers, the Dziennik Chicagoski. I can attest that many Poles and their descendants read this paper including my own ancestors. Recent immigrants may have been able to speak enough English to get around the town and their jobs, but often reading and writing English was not accomplished until their children went to school and were immersed in the language outside of the ethnic neighborhood. Therefore, the Polish newspaper was an important part of knowing what was happening in Chicago's Polonia community.

The PGSA divided their death index into two databases, the first covering 1890 to 1929 and the second covering 1930 to 1971: http://www.pgsa.org/database.php

The odds of finding an ancestor in either of these databases are good. The early death records contained biographical information about a few of the Poles who died then. It was mostly the wealthier Poles of the North Side who published obituaries in the Dziennik in the 1890s and 1900s.

The success rate increases as the years pass but eventually taper off with the 1950s and 1960s as people moved away from their ethnic identities and their associated papers. Your ancestor is virtually guaranteed to be in the Dziennik if he or she was wealthy or well connected in the Polish community. If your ancestor was an ordinary person, the odds of finding him or her from 1890 to 1910 are slim. From 1920 to 1950 the odds are excellent. From 1950 and later the chances are good but not great. At this time, the odds of finding older folks who were born in the late 1800s and were a part of Chicago's Polonia for many years are best. Finding younger folks (born as first- or second-generation Americans) will not be as successful in the later years of the paper, but still try to find them. The younger Poles moved out from Chicago to the suburbs and beyond and often did not subscribe to the newspaper of their parents and grandparents in favor of the English newspapers.

The typical Dziennik obituary will be in Polish, but do not let that be a deterrent. It has some good, easily translatable information. The PGSA has a downloadable guide to translating the entries. The typical obituary has the person's name, address of funeral (remember, people were waked in their living rooms in the early 1900s), place of burial, and names of living relatives. Here is the official translation guide: http://www.pgsa.org/PDFs/DzChicObit.pdf

The beauty of these indexes is that the people who indexed them (major kudos) also indexed the names of other people in the records for the early death entries and then spouses for the later entries. In other words, it is possible to find connections among people using these obituaries. These obituaries typically list extended family such as uncles, nieces, cousins, and any relatives who were prominent in that person's life.

I used these obituaries to solve some mysteries and prove a couple of familial relationships (backed up by other records, of course). This index led me to the discovery that my ggg-grandmother, Agnes Iglewski, was married twice, to Wojciech Mazgaj and then to Wojciech Mondrala. Peter Iglewski's death record showed Mondrala relatives and thus pointed me in the right direction to find these relatives.

I highly recommend using these databases because they contain a lot of wonderful information about the people in them. I also recommend ordering a photocopy of the actual obituary from the PGSA. The order form is on their website, and the fee is definitely worth it. The hard copy of the obituary is needed to gain the maximum amount of information: http://www.pgsa.org/dzien9029.php#copies

The other nice thing about using the PGSA database for obituaries is that your ancestor's name probably will be spelled correctly. This was a Polish paper for Polish people, so any misspellings would have been typos, not misunderstandings between two different cultures. Your search in the PGSA obituary databases will not take much time but will be very fruitful. The paper's final issue was in 1971, so unfortunately that is the last year to find any obituaries from the Dziennik, but by then so many people were English-speaking and immersed in the English-speaking world that post-1971 Dziennik entries probably would not have been common.

English Papers

I have searched and searched in vain for early death entries (1870-1940) in the English papers such as the Chicago Tribune with little success. The only Poles who published obituaries in those papers were wealthy, well-to-do Poles with many connections to the English-speaking community (such as through a big, successful business). In other words, most of the Poles in Chicago would not be listed in there.

The best that can be found is a notice of a death certificate being issued to a certain person. The Chicago Tribune published a list of burial permits that the city issued that day. Ancestry has digitized these entries from the Chicago Tribune. However, the database they created was obviously one of the first ones for their site, because it is awkward and clumsy to use with few fields to search for. It has trouble picking up the simplest of spelling changes such as "Stefanak" when searching "Stefaniak." I have not had much luck with ProQuest and other software that claims to have indexed Tribune and other newspapers from this era.

Finding these lists on microfilm copies of the Tribune from that particular day is easiest. Finding microfilmed copies of the turn-of-the-century Tribune is not easy. Simply put, the Chicago Tribune is not a good source for finding death information about your Polish ancestor. There are many superior databases for that. If your ancestor was listed in the lists mentioned above, then he or she definitely has a burial permit entry floating out there. A burial permit entry is easier to find than a Tribune entry. In other words, searching through the Tribune really isn't worth the time.

I think 1940 was the magic year that the faucet of Polish obituaries was turned on because after that year, many Polish people placed obituaries in the Chicago Tribune, which can easily be found by searching the Tribune's archives. If your ancestor died from 1950 onward, the odds are good. They may have an obituary in the Chicago Sun-Times or a smaller paper, but the Tribune is the best place to start because it has the most.

If you live in the Chicagoland area, try the local library; it probably has an online subscription to the Chicago Tribune. Search its historical archives in the obituary section. I have found that the children and grandchildren of immigrants are easily found in the Tribune's obituary archives. Ancestry has a name index for 1988 to 1997, but the full-text entries are in the 1986 full-text Tribune database that, hopefully, your local library has. Check both the Chicago Tribune and Chicago Sun-Times because both were major papers in the Chicago area. Ancestry's collection of obituaries is very good for the 2000s. Check Ancestry for recent obituaries. The local public library may also have an index of obituaries from local papers that may be useful.

B. Cemetery Records

Just as our Polish ancestors attended Polish churches, they also wanted to be buried in a Polish cemetery. The majority of Polish Chicagoans were buried in one of two Catholic cemeteries: St. Adalbert in Niles or Resurrection in Chicago. They were buried in other cemeteries, such as Holy Cross in South Chicago, Graceland in Chicago, and All Saints in Chicago, but the majority were buried in the first two mentioned. Finding the cemetery of burial is easy for later records; all death certificates had to list a cemetery of burial. Early vital records had to list a cemetery but often only "Polish cemetery" or "Bohemian cemetery" is listed on the early, pre-1900 Polish death certificates. Again, that usually meant St. Adalbert in Niles, but it could have meant a different cemetery.

Try St. Adalbert first, because it is the big daddy of Polish cemeteries. It is the oldest Polish cemetery, opened in 1872, and serviced the majority of the early Polish settlers of Cook County as well as the majority of inhabitants on the North Side of Chicago. Resurrection cemetery opened in 1904 and afterward became the cemetery of choice for South Side Poles. Therefore, before checking cemeteries, determine where your ancestors lived. It was rare to bury a South Side Pole in St. Adalbert Cemetery after 1904. I have found that even South Side widowed spouses would be buried in Resurrection after 1904 even if their husband or wife was buried in St. Adalbert.

Cemetery records are relatively good for Polish genealogy, compared to other areas, but still do not offer that much. Death certificates from Cook County or death records from churches have more information than cemetery records.

The Catholic Cemeteries of Chicago have informational kiosks with grave locations at every Catholic cemetery—check it to determine the exact cemetery your ancestors were buried. Be warned though, these kiosks are located inside the lobbies and thus are only available during the cemetery's business hours, which are normal weekday hours and Saturday mornings. Without the gravesite information, you will have little hope of finding your ancestor among the thousands and thousands of graves at each cemetery.

Even with the gravesite information, finding the grave will be difficult. Some parts of St. Adalbert have clear signs denoting cemetery sections, rows, and subdivisions. Other parts do not have good signage. The signage at Resurrection is almost non-existent, even for the new parts. It also takes some exercise to find your ancestor's grave, so bring water and wear walking shoes.

Older graves have upright headstones or even grand monuments with statues. In fact, some older graves even have photographs in them. Naturally my only ancestor with a photograph-included grave has only the slot left; his photograph is lost to the ages. Later graves are simple stones set flat in the ground. These later graves tend to sink and are obscured by ground; if a grave is terribly sunken, do not hesitate to tell the front-desk staff about it. Grave maintenance is part of the cemetery's duty.

Now, all of this is assuming that your ancestor had a headstone, which may not have been the case. The bane of Chicago Polish genealogists is called "term graves at St. Adalbert." The Polish custom was to bury someone in the village cemetery somewhere on the family's plot of land in that cemetery. The villages were small and everyone knew everyone, so there was no need to place a headstone or marker of a permanent nature in that spot. I asked a cousin who lived in Poland about where my gg-grandparents were buried in Szczawnica, Poland, and she said that they simply were buried in their family plot with their youngest child, who died in the 1970s, buried on top of them. There was no special marker for them; it was just the Gabrys family's grave.

This mentality continued into America and was compounded by the fact that headstones were (and still are) expensive. Few Polish families could afford large and fancy headstones, and many working-class Polish families couldn't even afford a permanent grave. Therefore, many people were buried in "term graves" at St. Adalbert. This practice was common in the late 1800s and will frustrate genealogists of the 2000s considerably.

Why is this so frustrating? Aside from the original notation of place of burial, the record trail stops. If a person was buried in a term grave, they had that spot of land for 25 years and then someone else was buried on top of them. That later person probably would put a headstone up, headstones being relatively cheaper in the 1900s, and thus the person underneath is completely forgotten.

Can't I just find the person using the original notation, you ask? The short answer is no. The original notation system used a coordinate system that the cemetery no longer uses. In fact, the cemetery staff I spoke to said that no one can locate graves using the old coordinates because those locations have been lost. The best they can do is to find a general area in the cemetery where that section probably was located. My relative, Peter Mroz, is buried in grave 504 of section VCH. The map of St. Adalbert has no section VCH listed anymore. Does St. Adalbert have some old records that might be able to help us? Possibly. However, I do not recommend asking them genealogical questions beyond, "I have the grave marker coordinates from the Catholic Directory—could you please take out a map of the section and show me where the grave is located?" They are concerned with recent burials and people planning future burials, not finding information about people who lived (and paid) decades ago.

Here is the long answer. It is possible to find your ancestor beyond the original term-grave entry. My example is my ggg-grandmother's second husband, Frank Mroz, your typical poor Polish peasant laborer. He came to Chicago in approximately 1870, worked in the lumber yards, and died in 1887 at the age of 47 of causes unknown (many death certificates from 1887 have been lost, including his). Frank was buried in a term grave and that was that. I almost gave up on him. However, I started searching for his wife, my ggg-grandmother, Marianna Janoska/Marcyanna Jozwiak. I found a Maryanna Mroz that could be her and saw that she was buried in a big plot with several people nearby. I asked the cemetery staff to see the sketch of the plot to see who was buried in it. Lo and behold, it was the Frank Mroz from the term grave, this time with new cemetery numbers that did not appear on the screen when I searched his name. I suspect that my ggg-grandmother purchased the term grave for him, spoke to her friends, the Wysockis, and they decided to fully purchase the plot on top of him and be buried next to him. Is the case the norm? Of course not. My point is to try every angle.

Also keep in mind that family members tended to be buried with each other, so they may have purchased the land around other burials. Search for all your ancestors; don't zero in on one or two. Search for as many as possible and always keep your eyes open at the cemetery. Relatives liked to be buried by each other, so look for some familiar names at the graves around your ancestor.

Infant mortality was a grim and ever-present reality to our ancestors. Women had large families, because they accepted the fact that many of their children would die before getting married—many in infancy or young childhood. Therefore, it is common to see a woman having eleven children of whom five survived to adulthood. Of those five, maybe three or four will produce children of their own. This is the case of the family of Valentine Stefaniak, my gg-grandfather, and is the case of most other Polish families of this era. If all of your ancestor's siblings or children survived to adulthood, then that would be the exception to the rule. I have never seen that before in the late 1800s—the closest being eight children surviving out of nine. And, of course, with miscarriages factored into that equation, the odds that all of a woman's children survived are almost zero.

The infants' sections of both cemeteries are vast fields filled with countless children and few markers showing the recent section names, which often do not coincide with the older section names. It is possible to get close to finding their location, but finding their exact gravesites is next to impossible. It is sad. It is unfortunate. But then it was seen as a fact of life; only the toughest, strongest children could survive a life without antibiotics and all of the other wonders of modern medicine. Families often had many miscarriages and could not afford fancy burials for every infant that died.

Cemetery markers themselves can be beautiful works of art. Some families had statues on top of or next to their headstones. Others had artwork etched onto the headstones. The wealthiest few built family mausoleums, which are small, indoor chambers that hold anywhere from four to twenty caskets. The Patka mausoleum at Resurrection Cemetery is one of my favorites; it is a stunning work of art. I could write a book on cemetery markers alone, so I will leave the art at that.

Cemetery markers are not the most reliable genealogical tools. The date of death should coincide with the death certificate (if a family could afford a headstone, then they most definitely would have had a death certificate). The date of birth is often wrong on headstones. The year is usually off and the day may or may not be accurate. Treat the information on gravestones cautiously and check it against other sources. The one gleeful moment that may happen in a cemetery is that there could be a photograph of your ancestor on his or her cemetery marker.

Resurrection Cemetery became the premier cemetery for South Side Poles after it opened in 1904. Both cemeteries have mostly upright markers in the old sections and mostly flat, on-the-ground markers in the new sections. Beautiful artistic graves can be seen at both. If you have Polish ancestry in Chicago, you will definitely be doing some searching at one or both of these cemeteries. St. Adalbert is mostly Slavic, but Resurrection is the resting place for many different nationalities.

Your Polish ancestors could have been buried in other Catholic cemeteries in the Chicagoland area. Some Poles, especially the early ones, were not buried at Catholic cemeteries. One of my gg-granduncle's children was buried at Graceland Cemetery in 1886. I suspect she was buried there because it was closer to home, and her grave could be visited more easily than St. Adalbert in Niles. When doing research at other cemeteries, check their websites to see research policies, what information is computerized, and what is not. Calling or emailing the cemetery before visiting to see if they can help locate your ancestor ahead of time.

Of course, after World War II, those of Polish descent fanned out across the Chicagoland area and were buried at a plethora of cemeteries ranging from Queen of Heaven in Hillside to Maryhill Cemetery in Niles. Finding recent burials definitely requires searching the all-cemetery-wide catalog in the lobby of all Catholic cemeteries in the Cook County area. That is the easiest and fastest way to find an ancestor. Your ancestor's death certificate will say which cemetery he or she was buried at, but it will not give the grave location, so still use the information kiosk in the cemetery lobby.

All in all, Polish cemetery research is not a daunting task. The majority of Poles are buried at St. Adalbert or Resurrection. Ask the staff to look up your ancestor's location on the maps they keep behind the desk, or head out to the section and try to locate the markers that give section and lot numbers. A word of caution: Often the finding aids are not the sections or are obscured by grass. Searching for graves can be challenging, but it is a rewarding experience.

Finding the remains of your ancestors is an emotional and moving experience. Bring some basic garden tools (or at least a pair of work gloves) to remove debris and grass that may have grown on your ancestors' graves. Don't forget water and good walking shoes. I also recommend going on a nice sunny day. The shadows help to read worn-away cemetery markers. Cemetery searching isn't the happiest experience, but it is a moving experience that is just as much a part of genealogy as finding census records is.

C. Funeral Home Records

I have read in several Polish genealogy publications that a person should check funeral homes for their records of who they have buried. Well, I'd like to know where the heck those people's ancestors were waked because Polish funeral parlors did not keep very detailed records at the time. I contacted all undertakers my ancestors used and, of those who still exist, none had records for burials that happened more than twenty or twenty-five years ago. Funeral home records are good for some locations but not in Chicago. The focus of this book is genealogy from 1860-1945, and there are virtually no funeral home resources left from this era for the Cook County Polish.

Any that still exist will exist within your family. A cousin of mine saved the funeral-home's bill from my great-granduncle's funeral in 1925. That is the only funeral-home record I have found and that will be something you will have found already having completed the research suggested in Chapter One. Outside of that, do not waste time searching for funeral-home records when death certificates and cemetery information tell the same thing and are quicker and easier to locate.

D. Mass Cards

Interesting and often overlooked genealogical resources are the mass cards that are handed out at funerals. This is a Catholic custom that became popular in the mid-twentieth century. I have funeral cards from dozens of burials, some related and some not. These are small cards about the size of a credit card that list the deceased's name, date of death, and a prayer for them. Sometimes it lists birthday, spouse, location of birth, or other information. They varied from funeral home to home. The early ones I have are from the 1940s and are written in Polish. The information on them can be found in other sources, but they are useful relics of our ancestors that are a constant reminder of their humanity.

CHAPTER SEVEN: CHICAGO AND MIDWESTERN RECORDS AND RESOURCES

1. Chicago Resources

A. Voter Registration Records

It is now time to research the special records. Chicago has a lot to offer in the way of Polish genealogy, and it also has some unique records to help us in our quest.

One such set of records is the Chicago Voter Registration records of 1888-1892. These records are the lists of citizens who registered to vote in the 1888, 1890, and 1892 elections. What makes these records special is that they cover a period that was destroyed by fire. The 1890 fire completely obliterated Cook County census, so it will not help us find our ancestors. The voter registration records from this period help make up for this loss.

The voter registration records record the name of the person who is about to vote, his or her home address, country of origin, time at that particular home address, time living in Illinois, time in the United States, date of naturalization, and place of naturalization if not a natural-born citizen. Do I even need to devote a sentence to how wonderful finding this record would be for your genealogical research? These records can be accessed on Ancestry or on microfilm from LDS.

The 1890 and 1892 voter registration records are in relatively good condition. The 1888 records are in rougher shape and contain many pages that once held information but have since become illegible. Therefore, begin your search with the 1890 voter records, and after some experience working these records, move back to the trickier 1888 records. I used this technique and found my gg-grandmother's brother, Ignatz Jozwiak, in all of them. I found my gg-grandfather, Valentine Stefaniak, in 1890 and 1892 but not 1888.

However, to find your ancestor, make sure that he was naturalized (remember, women weren't legally able to vote in national elections at this time). Locate your ancestor in the 1900 census first because this will provide some naturalization information. Again, the naturalization information on censuses is not perfect, but it can give an idea of when it happened. Unfortunately, my gg-grandfather Michael Pietrzak was naturalized in 1893 and thus would not be found in any of these records because only naturalized citizens are eligible to vote.

These records are excellent aids that can help locate your ancestors' ship records. I have found that the information in them is very accurate—even better than census records. They can determine whether your ancestor lived anywhere other than Illinois after coming to America. Also, finding your ancestor's address is very important. Remember how I said before that often the address on the birth certificate or death certificate is the only means of proving that person was related to your ancestor? Bingo. Here is proof of address in 1890, thus providing information for that frustrating period between the 1880 census and 1900 census.

Search Ancestry's index first. The problem with this index is that the images are not browsable. I contacted Ancestry regarding this, and they said that this is due to the contract that they have with the record keepers. The handwriting is relatively good, so transcription issues aren't the biggest problem. Misspellings on the original records are. My two big examples are Valentine Stefaniak AKA Walenty Stephanick in 1890, AKA Val Stepanicki in 1892 and then Ignatz Jozwiak AKA Ignatz Jozniak in 1888, AKA Ignatz Joznick in 1890, and triumphantly Ignatz Jozwiak in 1892.

Out of five examples, one was spelled correctly. The transcriptions were beautiful; the original records were wrong. Why is that? Much has to do with our ancestors' literacy. I know that Ignatz was literate, but I do not think Valentine was. If someone cannot read, write, and spell well (especially in a language that is not the native tongue), then errors are bound to happen when an American clerk takes down his or her information.

If the search on Ancestry is not successful, then turn to the microfilm records of LDS. These records cover a small percentage of the population in Chicago, naturalized and native-born adult males. You will not have to sift through 100,000 possibilities like you could with census records. Persistence and determination will pay off in the search for this uniquely Chicago record that will help considerably in your search.

B. City Directories

City directories are a fairly good source for genealogy in Chicago. Like most other records, the longer your family has been in America, the more likely you are to find them in city directories. Dozens of city directories have been published for the city of Chicago and some include other areas of Cook County. Look at each individual volume to see which towns and municipalities are included.

The best place to find data on city directories is the Newberry Library website -- www.chicagoancestors.org -- along with in-person research at either the Chicago History Museum or the Newberry Library. To find the city directories on the Newberry Library website, click "tools" at the top of the page There will be two lists: the first list contains the business directories available online; the second list contains the personal directories available online. If your ancestor owned a business, check out the business directories, but they will not be useful for the majority of Polish researchers. Not many Poles owned their own businesses in this time; I only have a few relatives who did, but the business directories are a great resource for such research.

Chicago Ancestors contains city directories from 1866 until 1923. It also has a link detailing other directories published in that time frame, along with which city directories can be found at the Newberry library. The Newberry Library has many tomes from many parts of the country, so I recommend browsing this full list before visiting. The other directories typically won't be of use to Polish-American genealogists because our ancestors had their own societies (typically centered on the church) with their own publications that had no connection with the city's official publications.

Personal city directories are easy to use. Click the year of interest and then click the first letter of the surname of the person being researched. This navigation is in Adobe Acrobat Reader, but it feels like web surfing. If you do not have Adobe Reader, please— by all means—put down this book and download it immediately. This free and excellent software is useful in all facets of the internet.

Begin the search using the city directories published on the Newberry Library's website. They purposely have at least one directory for each decade from the 1860s to the

1920s. The information listed depends on the directory, but typically the head of the household will be listed along with his profession and address. It will probably give his occupation as well. Women are rarely listed; the Polish women that I have found in city directories had non-domestic jobs (dressmaking, for example) and therefore will only be listed if they wanted other people to contact them for business purposes.

City directories can help you find your ancestors in census records. If you can't find your ancestor in the 1910 census but can in the 1910 city directory, then the odds are that he was living in the same place. Look up this place using the enumeration district finder discussed earlier on Stephen Morse's website and then browse the images on Ancestry.

City directories are good for tracking the migration of a family from one house to another. Poles moved around a bit before getting settled in America, so your ancestors probably lived at three, four, or five addresses before purchasing a home. Finding the correct address helps verify the identity of people in birth and death records, too.

One thing to keep in mind is the address changes that happened in Chicago in 1909 and 1911. Also, street names in Chicago changed at different points in the city's history. Conversion guides for the old numbering system as well as for old street names can be found in this spot on the Newberry Library's website. These are handy tools that should be downloaded by anyone interested in Chicago genealogy. Converting addresses is useful to verify the identity of someone in a pre-1916 vital record.

Don't hold your breath when sifting through the city directories of the 1870s; however, the odds of finding your ancestor in a city directory from the 1900s and later are good. City directories are just one more tool in Chicago's genealogical toolkit.

C. Chicago Property Records

Making a list of addresses where your ancestor lived is a good way to track and organize your ancestor's movement throughout Chicago. Looking at the history of these houses can be fun as well. More information about your ancestor is found by looking at his or her home but only if you are willing to navigate the Cook County bureaucracy through a trip downtown.

Before attempting any research of the kind about to be detailed, please make sure that your ancestors actually owned the home where they lived. Poles often rented, especially in the early years of settling Chicago, before they could afford to buy a house. Renters probably will not show up in the following records. Look at census records to see if he or she owned the home. A column on all census records from 1900 to 1930 says whether the head of household owned the home (with a mortgage or free and clear) or whether the home was rented. Search for the magic letters O/F/M, not R, before proceeding on to this type of research. R stands for rented while O stands for owned; F and M stood for whether a house was owned free and clear or whether it was owned but with a mortgage payment, respectively.

Property records are stored at the Cook County Recorder of Deeds office and the Cook County Assessor's Office in the Cook County Building in downtown Chicago. Recent properties are in the Recorder of Deeds office, so it won't help with researching for the time frame covered in this book (plus there records have more restrictions about their use). Searching in the Cook County Assessor's Office in the basement of the County Building is a better option.

Before going to either place, find the property's PIN. This can be found at the Cook County Assessor's website: http://cookcountyassessor.com/. Make sure to have the full address and PIN clearly written. Then get in line, tell the clerk your intent, and he or she will punch in the information and refer you to a ledger book kept in the vast bookcases filled with information about that particular piece of property.

All of this sounds wonderful, but honestly, property records are not that great. They are bureaucratic and legal in nature, not genealogical. They are filled with symbols, abbreviations, and terminology that are just plain confusing, even with the guide sheets provided. Yes, the owners of that property are listed along with the years they owned it, but this information is limited. If your ancestors lived in a particular house for decades (and thus it has become dear to your heart), then find its PIN, go downtown, and sift through the legal mumbo jumbo. It's a nifty little record. Its value is relative to the seeker, but it may be worth your while to do some searching.

D. Probate Records

Virtually all genealogy books devote time to discussing probate records and how wonderful they are for genealogists. Well, that is true for many people; however, I cannot say the same for Polish–Americans in Cook County. I have sifted through the probate indexes of Cook County and have found few Polish surnames in the records.

Probate records are found either on microfilm from LDS or in person at the archives of the Cook County Circuit Court. I recommend the latter simply because the county's indexes cover a greater time span than LDS, and they are all in one location rather than being scattered across many rolls of microfilm.

Searching the indexes is fairly standard. There are a few microfilm readers in the archives, so find the roll of microfilm with the year that your ancestor died, and then scroll through the microfilm to see whether he or she (usually he) is listed.

Keep in mind that everyone did not go through probate when they died. Probate court was only called in (during this time period) if there was a dispute in inheritance among the heirs or if a person's total assets were worth a great deal of money. Many people did not have this kind of money, so they will not be found in probate. Even if they owned their own homes, if the family did not feud about who became the next owner of the property, then probate would not have been necessary.

The actual probate records are not kept on location at the archives in the Daley Center. Fill out the order form at the archives and then wait the week or so that it takes to order the records from the warehouse and transport them to the archives for viewing. After that, these records are free to view inside the archives, but they charge for making photocopies.

Typically these records are held together with metal clips and are on thin legal-sized paper. Finding an ancestor in probate is a veritable genealogical goldmine simply because probate court had to find out the potential heirs of that person ranging from children to cousins to nieces and nephews. Need I say more? Definitely order the original probate record if an ancestor is in one of the indices.

Like all other records, the later the year, the easier it is to find an ancestor. I have found only one ancestor in probate records, my gg-grandmother's sister, Frances Szarzynski, maiden name Chmiel. I found her because she had no biological children but had purchased some bonds before she died that needed to be divided among her heirs. Therefore, the probate record listed not only her nieces and nephews in the United States but also all known relatives in Poland! Granted, the witnesses who testified did not know whether many of these people were still living, it was still a genealogical gold mine to see all of those names that I had never seen before. I believe the informant was her brother-in-law, my gg-grandfather, Michael Pietrzak. He would have been more than eighty years old at the time, so he was probably wheeled into the room and asked for a Polish-to-English translator.

Probate records are wonderful sources of information for Americana ancestry and for wealthy immigrant ancestry. By all means, go to the Cook County Circuit Court Archives and search through the indexes, but please do not get frustrated or angry. The odds are fairly bad. Finding someone in a probate record will be an amazing find, not a typical find.

E. Legal Records

Obtaining a copy of a court document is the same process as obtaining a copy of a probate record. The indexes for legal records are found in the archives of the circuit court, just like probate records. Order them in the same way. They organized the same as probate records—held together with metal clips on legal-sized paper.

That being said, not many Poles generated court records such as divorces, guardianship motions, and other court documents of the like. Don't spend too much time in these indexes unless you know that one of your relatives was divorced or had some kind of legal proceedings. Keep in mind that many Poles could not afford lawyers and therefore did not generate the legal records that richer people may have.

Another thing to keep in mind is that these are county court records. The federal government holds all federal court records, so a trip to the National Archives and Records Administration (NARA) is necessary for conducting research at the federal level. The Great Lakes facility in Chicago holds all of those records and indexes along with federal naturalization records. It is worth a visit to see whether your ancestors may have ended up in federal court. Why would they have landed in federal court? Well, they may have violated Prohibition as my gg-grandmother's brother did. Michael Mazgaj violated federal law, was tried in federal court, and thus generated documentation found only at NARA.

Search in the court indexes that are available. There may be something, but don't get your hopes up too high; court documents are not in the ancestry file of many Polish Americans between 1860 and 1945.

F. Coroner's Inquest Files

Finding a death certificate in the late nineteenth century is not always possible. It is easier than finding birth records but harder than finding marriage records. Yet, for some people, it is impossible to find a death certificate. One reason may be that they had a Coroner's Death Certificate and not a Cook County Death Certificate. Only the latter is available on the LDS website.

If a question arose in the death of your ancestor, or if he or she died by unnatural means, then the Cook County coroner would have gotten involved in the case. If the coroner was involved, then an investigation would be mounted in the death and a jury would decide on what the final cause of death was and who (if anyone) was responsible for that person's death.

Cook County Coroner's inquest files are excellent documents that can yield great genealogical information. The records from 1872 to 1911 are indexed, and this database is at: http://www.cyberdriveillinois.com/departments/archives/cookinqt.html

This database is easy to use; type in the first few letters of your ancestor's surname and the search results will return anything that starts with those letters. These records have many spelling mistakes, so doing a broad search may pay off. After finding an ancestor in this database, print the information and mail it to the Illinois Regional Archives Depository (IRAD) at Northeastern Illinois University requesting a photocopy of this record. They will mail the photocopy along with a bill for a nominal photocopying charge. More details can be found at the above link.

In reality a coroner's inquest file is simply a certificate from the coroner listing the result of the inquest. It will have the name of the decedent, date of death, address of death, final cause of death as determined by the jury, two witnesses to the decedent, their addresses, and whether the decedent had any unresolved property of value that needed to be passed on to any heirs. The witnesses were usually relatives or physicians who attended to the decedent. These useful records give a final cause of death. They also point the way to the coroner's death certificate, which lists the same information as the inquest file just in a different format. Coroner's death certificates are not online yet; they can only be obtained directly from Cook County or from the LDS microfilms of them.

Now this is all true for coroner's inquest files before 1911. If your ancestor had an inquest after 1911, then obtaining a copy of that file is harder but definitely worth the time and effort. After 1911, there were no coroner's death certificates, only county death certificates, so that obstacle is removed. There is no easy way to find out whether your ancestor had an inquest between 1911 and 1916 short of contacting the Cook County Coroner's office and asking them to do a manual search of their files. For post 1916 death certificates, look on the right side of the death certificate; there is a box that says "I hereby certify that I ...." There will then be three choices after that sentence: inquiry, inquest, and autopsy. If inquiry was selected, then there is no other information available. If inquest was selected, then the Cook County Coroner's office will have a file relating to that individual. If inquiry was selected, then there is no other information available. If an autopsy was performed, then there may or may not be some more information available. Check the Coroner's office to see if any is available.

If an inquest was held, contact the Cook County Coroner for a copy of the case file. Be warned: There is a long wait time. Call them, explain the situation to the operator, and hopefully be transferred to someone who will help. Remember, the coroner's office's main priority is murder victims and other such incidents that are happening today, not eighty years ago. Genealogical searches are low on their list of priorities.

A good strategy to use is to both call them and submit a request in writing. They will search for your ancestor eventually, but it will not be cheap. Six months and more than forty dollars later, I obtained a copy of my great-grandfather's brother's inquest file. His name was Lawrence Kruszka, and he died in an industrial accident. I got not only the sheet detailing the final verdict the jury reached but also a transcript of the hearing. The hearing was held so that legal representatives of his company could bring forth witnesses to testify to the coroner how exactly my relative reached his death. This testimony was fascinating but also held genealogical pay dirt, because in the beginning, they questioned his wife as to where her husband came from, who his parents were, whether he had any prior medical conditions, and the like. It was well worth the money.

Be patient with the coroner's office; it took six months for them to process my request. However, it was worth the wait. Coroner's inquest files are excellent pieces of information.

G. Delayed Birth Certificates

A delayed birth certificate was filed some time after the child was born. It has documentary evidence such as a baptismal record or sworn affidavit that the child was born at that time. Some counties, such as Cook County, have good delayed birth records but others do not.

A person usually filed a delayed birth certificate request if he or she was trying to get married or get a social security number but had no civil birth record. This index is mostly made up of people who filed in the 1930s and 1940s and were born between 1890 and 1930. The LDS Church has microfilmed the delayed birth index, but it has not microfilmed the original records of these elusive delayed births.

It's tough to say why a regular birth certificate was not filed at the time of birth. Your ancestor almost certainly was born at home with a midwife rather than in a hospital with a physician. Hospitals kept strict records versus midwives who were supposed to keep records but often did not.

That being said, these records are elusive. First, locate your ancestor in the index. This is not found online; order the roll of microfilm from LDS that has this title and then pick the roll of microfilm that contains your ancestor's surname. Hopefully that roll of microfilm lists your ancestor. Here are the microfilm listings for Cook County delayed birth records:
https://www.familysearch.org/search/catalog/show?uri=http%3A%2F%2Fcatalog-search-api%3A8080%2Fwww-catalogapi-webservice%2Fitem%2F263696

Although it is probably easier to go to www.familysearch.org, click on "Catalog" and then type in "Cook County Delayed Births."

That was the easy part. The tricky part is obtaining a copy of that delayed birth record. These records are not found online in the LDS collection of Cook County birth records, so order them directly from Cook County. However, the employees will search for your ancestor's record in the collection of normal birth certificates, so be sure to attach a letter of explanation to the order form. I suggest taking a photograph of the actual index that has your ancestor in it, attaching this photograph to your search request form, and writing a short letter explaining that your ancestor's birth record is found in the "delayed" birth certificates of Cook County, not the regular birth certificates.

This is the technique that I used with my grandfather's birth record. For some reason, out of four children, he was the only one who did not have a birth certificate filed when he was born. I was very frustrated that I could not find his birth certificate until I checked the delayed birth index, and sure enough, it was there, filed in 1941, the year he married my grandmother. I suspect that Cook County asked for a government-issued birth certificate in order to give him a marriage license, so he filed for a delayed record to fulfill this requirement. I followed the steps outlined above, and, sadly, Cook County sent me a letter saying they could not find it. Yet, a week later, I received another letter with the birth certificate attached. It makes me wonder whether the first person who looked at my request did not actually read it but another person realized the first's mistake.

This is a lot more of a hassle than can normally be expected from a simple birth certificate request, but trust me, it is well worth the effort. This is a great way to nail down the names, dates, and facts needed in your family tree for those relatives who are tricky to find.

2. Midwestern Research

Researching Polish ancestry in other Midwestern states is much like researching Polish ancestry in Illinois. Begin with documents found in the home, work up to census records, and search Ancestry and Family Search for relevant resources. After that, contact the county building for the county that your ancestors lived in to find out which vital records survive and where they are housed. Cook County has a lot to offer Polish–Americans, but there is a lot to discover in states such as, Indiana, Michigan, Minnesota, Wisconsin, and the other areas where Poles settled.

Indiana

Many Poles migrated eastward from Chicago to northwest Indiana, drawn in by the booming steel industry at the beginning of the twentieth century. If a person vanishes off of the radar after 1910 or 1920, check for him or her in Indiana. That is how I solved two of my genealogical mysteries. One relative moved to Porter County, Indiana, and another moved to Elkhart, Indiana.

The PGSA has some Indiana records in its databases, but the best place to find Indiana resources is on Ancestry and Family Search. Family Search has an indexing project that is working to index all Indiana marriages from 1811 to 1959, and it is slowly working its way toward the counties that had large Polish populations such as Lake County.

The Polish cemeteries of northwest Indiana do not have a central archive like the Catholic cemeteries of Chicago, so finding the grave of an ancestor in Indiana is more difficult than in Illinois. However, some people chose to be buried in Holy Cross cemetery in South Chicago; if that is the case, their information will be found in the Catholic cemeteries of Chicago database. St. Joseph and St. Michael cemeteries were the popular choices in northwest Indiana for Poles to be buried in. The records from these cemeteries are not as complete as the records from Chicago Catholic cemeteries, so be sure to contact the cemeteries and explain what you are looking for to the operator who can help you in your particular case.

Michigan

Michigan has had a large Polish population since the 1860s. Early Polish settlers came to the Bay City region, Detroit, and other urban areas. The best guide to Polish genealogy in Michigan is to begin with the Polish Genealogical Society of Michigan: http://www.pgsm.org/

The website contains links to some Polish churches and cemeteries along with information about the society and when it meets.

Family Search has millions of vital records from Michigan on its website that are free to search along with Michigan indexing projects. Michigan's 1894 census has been indexed, but the images are not available to view. Ancestry has even more records from Michigan that can be found here:

http://search.ancestry.com/Places/US/Michigan/Default.aspx

Many Poles moved from Michigan in the latter half of the twentieth century, but to this day, there are still thousands of people of Polish descent living and thriving in Michigan.

Minnesota

Relatively speaking, not many Poles settled in Minnesota, but those who did usually became farmers. Searching for them in the territorial and state censuses of Minnesota is the best place to start. These are found on Ancestry. Family Search has more Minnesota collections than Indiana and Michigan, but it does not currently have any Minnesota indexing projects.

The PGSA recently released a database of birth records from parishes in Minnesota that contain Polish surnames. The odds of finding a Polish Minnesotan in this database are good. There is also a Minnesota marriage indexing project at Family Search in order to create a free, searchable database of Minnesota marriages which will eventually contain all those of Polish descent.

An excellent starting point for Minnesota research is found on Rootsweb at http://www.rootsweb.ancestry.com/~mngenweb/

Wisconsin

Wisconsin has had a large Polish population ever since the mid-1800s. It also has a large metropolitan area that attracted many Polish immigrants, Milwaukee. A lot of Poles from the Prussian partition, West Prussia, Silesia, and eastern Poland, came to Milwaukee for many of the same reasons as going to Chicago—a large urban area with plenty of manufacturing job opportunities and the chance for societal advancement.

The PGSA has some databases dedicated to Milwaukee including an indexing project for the obituaries in the *Kuryer Polski*, Milwaukee's version of the *Dziennik Chicagoski* newspaper. You can obtain a copy of an obituary from this index by contacting the Milwaukee Public Library system. They charge $5 per obituary, but the service is prompt and very thorough, so I highly recommend taking advantage of it.

A researcher specializing in Milwaukee research is Al Wierzba. His blog it at http://polishamericangenealogy.blogspot.com/ and contains a lot of information about Polish ancestry in Wisconsin.

The difference between Catholic cemeteries in Chicago and Milwaukee is that the Milwaukee cemeteries actually have a website to conduct cemetery searches at http://www.cemeteries.org/genealogy.asp

Another place to search for Polish ancestry in Wisconsin is Portage County. Many Poles settled there along with Milwaukee. Once again, the best place to search for Polish ancestry in Wisconsin is on Ancestry and Family Search. Once those resources have been exhausted, turn to Wisconsin's genealogical societies to see if they can offer any help with your specific region in Wisconsin.

CHAPTER EIGHT: MISCELLANEOUS RECORDS

A. Social Security Number Applications

A nifty record that few genealogical resources mention is the application that our ancestors completed when applying for their social security numbers. Those records have been preserved on microfilm for posterity, and there is an organized way to order copies of them. It gets better—recently this method was put online, so the whole order can be placed with a credit card. Of all the government bureaucracy to deal with in genealogy, this is one of the best in terms of ease and practicality.

When our grandfathers, great-grandfathers, and everyone else applied for social security numbers in the 1930s and 1940s, they became a part of one of the largest government bureaucracies in existence. Therefore, they had to provide information to prove their identity. Before the government awarded a social security number, a person had to provide his or her first, middle, and last names; address; employer; age; birthday; place of birth; full name of father and mother; and a signature.

This information can be found in other places for other people, but keep in mind that the people applying for social security numbers using this type of application were not young. They were middle-aged workers; many were immigrants. If you cannot find a baptism or birth record for your ancestor using the means outlined above, then this is a great resource. Most applications list more than just the country of birth; it also may list the town of birth as well.

Here is the website: https://secure.ssa.gov/apps9/eFOIA-FEWeb/internet/main.jsp This site offers four options. There are two types of records to choose from and then a different price for each of those two options based on whether or not a social security number is provided, thus four different options and four different prices). A computer transcription of the record can be purchased if you provide social security number or if you do not. Do not order this record. It does not give all of the information found on the original application record. Besides, genealogists want original documents, not cheap transcriptions.

A record useful for genealogy is the "Photocopy of the Original Application for a Social Security Card." Yes, it is a relatively expensive record at $27 if a social security number is provided and $29 if it is not. I would not recommend purchasing this record for every ancestor in your family tree. However, I highly recommend this record for who are difficult to find information about. It is also a good tool that tells where your ancestor worked circa 1935 that also has a copy of his or her signature on it, if he or she received a social security number as an adult.

Now the prerequisite to this record is finding out whether your ancestor had a social security number. No number means no form was filled out. This information will be found on all death certificates from 1940 onward. In the beginning, it was mostly men getting social security numbers. Once children started receiving social security numbers at birth, then equal representation of the genders began. Also, younger to middle-aged people were more likely to have social security numbers than older, retired people.

B. Social Security Death Index

A decedent's social security number is listed in the Social Security Death Index after he or she died, so this is where to find a social security number without a copy of the death certificate. This index is found on many genealogical websites. The one on www.rootsweb.com seems to be updated more frequently than the one on Ancestry or FamilySearch. If a person is found in this index, then he or she definitely had a social security number, which would be listed in that record.

This index covers deaths from 1962 onward. A few are listed before 1962 (remember, there are no absolutes in genealogy), but do not count on it. From the 1960s onward, begin your search for death records with this amazing tool—another high point of government bureaucracy. This easy-to-use tool gives several facts about a deceased person: dates of birth and death, last zip code of residence, and social security number. The birthday information is less than reliable, but the rest is pure gold.

Keep in mind that in the latter half of the twentieth century, more and more older people moved south after retiring and may have died in a state such as Florida or Arizona. Therefore, there will be no death certificate in Cook County (although there may be an obituary in a newspaper such as the Tribune). Because this index is nationwide, deceased people can still be found regardless of where they died. It can also help answer a question that can plague genealogists: Is this person still alive? Name spellings are generally good in this index. After all, this index reflects the official name your ancestor went by in official documents, so it should be spelled correctly.

One variable with this index is retired railroad workers. This group had its own system of social security numbers and is listed as such in this index. Instead of a state issuing their social security numbers, it says "Long-time or retired railroad workers" in that column along with a number that reflects the railroads, not the state in which the social security number was issued.

Another thing to keep in mind is that a person's social security number was based upon where they were living at the time they applied for it. More information about how a person received a specific number sequence can be found on the government's social security website: http://www.ssa.gov/history/ssn/geocard.html

C. Railroad Records

The previous paragraph is the perfect transition to another hidden and virtually unknown resource for genealogists—railroad records. If your ancestor worked for a railroad company, then there may still be employment records that are of genealogical significance.

Before beginning your search, the exact name of the railroad your ancestor worked for is needed. Walking into the National Archives and telling the staff that your ancestor worked for "the railroad" probably will not yield many results. The name of the railroad may be found in death certificates and sometimes in census records.

Most notably, the records of the Pullman Corporation still exist and can be accessed by researchers. Begin research for Pullman records in the Newberry Library. In the Chicago area, the South Suburban Genealogical Society holds many of these records..

These records can be gold mines for certain employees. For more information about what these records offer, check out this society's website: http://www.ssghs.org/pullman

Many other railroad companies' employment records still exist but are not as famous as the Pullman records. Another resource to use is the US Railroad Retirement Board which will perform genealogical searches for a fee at http://www.rrb.gov/mep/genealogy.asp

Perform a quick Internet search on your ancestor's particular railroad to see what is out there. After that, contact the Newberry Library. The staff there is knowledgeable about records such as this and can find resources for certain railroads with records that still exist.

D. Employment Records

Aside from the railroads, few employment records from the early twentieth century are intact. It is worth a shot to search for these records, but do not get your hopes up. Begin a search for employment records at the Newberry Library and then the Chicago History Museum. Their researchers can help find whether a company's records still exist.

Sadly, the employment records of the Chicago Stockyards were destroyed when the Stockyards closed in 1971, but the University of Illinois at Chicago has a large collection of original documents relating to the Stockyards. I did not find any names of my relatives in them, but there were thousands of names stretched across dozens of file folders. Finding an ancestor in an original document such as that would definitely enhance a family tree.

Few employment records are left, but maybe that company left behind paperwork that mentions an ancestor of yours. Get creative and search for what is left.

E. Jubilee Book Entries

Finding the correct names, dates, and facts is a must in genealogy. However, remember that these names, dates, and facts belong to real people who lived, breathed, and laughed just as people today do. Some people have family portraits, personal diaries, and anecdotes about their ancestors to share. Some people (such as me) have things to share. I am a genealogist who longs to find out what kind of people his ancestors were beyond who they married, how many children they had, where they were employed, and more.

The Jubilee Book database, created by volunteers, is a project that indexed so-called "jubilee books" for various parishes across the United States. A jubilee book is a book published by a church to celebrate a landmark anniversary such as the fiftieth anniversary of the founding of a parish: http://www.pgsa.org/Jubilee.php

These books are more than just parish histories. They also include pages dedicated to early founders of the church and important people throughout the church's history. The information in these books is invaluable and unpredictable. Some books have lists of active parishioners; others have names of people who donated money to the church. Some have group photographs of clubs and organizations whereas others have photographs that parish members submitted. My point is that anything can show up in a jubilee book.

Jubilee books are excellent sources of photographs. I received photographs of relatives that I never would have obtained had I not searched the PGSA's Jubilee Book Index. If you find your ancestor's name in the database, there will be a code next to the name saying whether that name was found in a list, a biography, a photograph caption, or the like. Then, print out the order form and buy a photocopy of the page containing your ancestor's information from the Polish Museum of America (PMA).

The jubilee books are full of surprises, so it's worth a shot to search for all of your ancestors. The more prominent they were in the parish or the more activities they did, the more likely they are to appear in a book. This unique database could yield some information that transforms those names, dates, and facts into human beings.

CHAPTER NINE: DETERMINING THE POLISH VILLAGE OF ORIGIN

Let's jump across the ocean to where your family originated. Many different places can reveal where your ancestors originated. Finding the village of origin is critical. Without a specific place of origin, the odds of tracing your family tree beyond the shores of America are incredibly slim.

I use the term "village" in this chapter simply as a generic term to denote a place of origin for your ancestor. The fact is that your ancestor could have come from a rural farming village, a rural town, or an urban area. The majority of Polish immigrants came from the rural countryside, so village is the most appropriate term.

1. Ship Records

A. Early Ship Records: 1850-1900

Few ship records before 1900 recorded a village of origin. Surprisingly, the ship record of my step-ggg grandfather, Peter Mroz, did. In the place-of-origin column on his 1869 ship record, the word "Niemziech" was written. I didn't recognize it at first, but another record pointed me toward his village of origin, Niemczyn, Kozielsko, Poznan. I scanned further in the ship record and saw that more villages were recorded for people including Tremessen for one passenger, a village of origin for a different branch of my family (Trzemeszno, Mogilno, Poznan.) Sadly, this is the exception, not the rule. Out of my early ship records, only one ship record actually did record the village of origin for nineteenth century records.

The emigration records for the port of Hamburg recorded a village of origin for the people who passed through there. These records were kept in German and recorded the information of the emigrants who were leaving the European continent for the British Isles, Canada, and America. The majority of Poles left through Bremen, so the odds of finding someone listed in the Hamburg records are slim. Take a look at all ship records you have with your ancestors' names to see if they left from Bremen, Hamburg, or a different port. If their ship left Hamburg, then this information will be an excellent way to find a village of origin.

As of this writing, Ancestry has only indexed years 1877 through 1914 but has the images from 1850 to 1934. Sifting through the images is worth it if your ancestor definitely came via Hamburg before 1877. A sea voyage took a couple weeks to complete, depending upon whether the ship was on a direct voyage from Hamburg to America or an indirect voyage from Hamburg to England or Ireland and then to America. My gg-grandmother Catherine Jozwiak left Hamburg on July 11, 1874, on her indirect voyage and arrived in America on July 29, 1874. That should give an idea of how long a voyage took and will help with sifting through the images on Ancestry.

The Hamburg passenger lists may or may not list the village that your ancestor came from, but they will definitely give the county. In the case of my gg-grandmother, it lists "Wagrowiec" as her place of origin instead of Starezyn, the village near Wagrowiec that she was born in. Although the village may not be listed, a county of origin is better than nothing.

Emigration records from other ports are spotty at best. Emigration records from Antwerp, Netherlands, do not exist, but police records do and may list your ancestor. These are records that were created to track the movement of foreigners who spent extended periods of time in the city. If your ancestor wanted to earn some money before traveling overseas, then he or she would probably be found in this database. Check for these records on Family Search.

Gdansk, Poland, was a port of emigration for late emigrants (1930s-1950s). U.S. customs lists from this port are easily accessible on Ancestry.

Most emigration records from Bremen, Germany, were destroyed, some by German authorities seeking to clear more space for recent records and some by American airmen during World War II. Information from these lists can be found on the American ship records for these voyages, but they did not record the village of origin as the Hamburg emigration records did.

The records kept by American customs officials are intact and are freely searchable on Ancestry for all sorts of ports from New York City to New Orleans to San Francisco. Canadian records from this time are also found on Ancestry and record virtually the same information as American ship records. Records before the 1900s do not tell much, but their format did vary so there may be some information on it.

B. Later Ship Records: 1900 and Onward

The information found on ships' manifests increased as time wore on. Ships have been recording the country of origin for their passengers since the early 1800s, but it was not until the early 1900s that ship records recorded the last residence of the passengers. This column will contain the place that the passenger lived in last, which usually will be a village of origin for him or her. The majority of immigrants came through Ellis Island at the turn of the twentieth century, and these records can be accessed at www.ellisisland.org or on Ancestry. Ellis Island's site requires registration, but it is otherwise freely searchable.

Also keep in mind that your ancestor may have come via Canada. If that is the case, then there will be a less detailed Canadian ship record for him or her on Ancestry along with a border crossing record (usually at St. Albans station in Vermont) that will contain much more information. Both of these types of records are searchable on Ancestry. Family Search has an indexing project for the ship records but not for the border crossing records.

The best ship records came from the 1910s and 1920s when they recorded the nearest living relative in the last place of residence. That is a great tool to see who the emigrant was leaving behind, and by extension, who was still alive at the time, be it a father, mother, brother, and such.

If your ancestor arrived after 1900, then a ship record is the best place to search for a village of origin. Before that time, ship records are relatively difficult to find and do not yield as much information as the later records do.

2. Birth and Death Certificates: Post-1916

Early vital records of Cook County did not list a village of origin, only a country or a region such as "Posen." However, a village of origin for a parent may have been listed on a child's birth certificate after 1916. Often only the country was recorded, but on some records, a village was recorded as well. Cross your fingers and hope that the record keeper was diligent and detailed.

The same goes for death records. A death certificate before 1910 asks for the birthplace of the decedent and his or her parents, but only a country will be given. A death certificate between 1910 and 1916 also asks for the birthplace of the decedent and his or her parents, but a region may be given instead of just the country. Death certificates after 1916 may give more detailed information but do not have to. The record keeper should have recorded the town or city of origin for the deceased and parents but rarely did. Often only "Poland" or "Posnania" was recorded.

Sometimes a country was recorded and sometimes a village was recorded from 1916 onwards. I have found death certificates that do not list parents or places of origin. I have found death certificates denoting the different origins of parents and the deceased person. This is probably the easiest method to finding a village of origin.

3. Church Records

Rarely did church records record a place of origin other than Chicago or Poland. However, some churches had beautiful record keeping, as earlier stated, and those included two big Polish Catholic churches, Stanislaus Kostka and Holy Trinity.

The church record that usually records place of origin is the marriage record. Few death records include place of origin, but some of Holy Trinity and Stanislaus Kostka's records do. There are very few microfilmed baptism records in Cook County that record the village of origin for the parents. Some later entries may, but generally baptism records are not where to find a village of origin.

The marriage records of Stanislaus Kostka are beautiful. They are legible, detailed, and include some place of origin for the bride and groom from the 1880s onward, gradually becoming more detailed as the years pass.

Once again, check the PGSA website (www.pgsa.org) to see if any of your ancestors were married in Stanislaus Kostka or Holy Trinity. Also be sure to check whether any siblings or cousins of your ancestors did. I found the village of origin for my direct ancestors, the Pietrzak family, by finding the marriage record of Thomas Szarzynski, a step-nephew of my gg-grandmother, and Frances Mrochin in Stanislaus Kostka.

4. Poznan Project, Pomorze, Geneteka, and Przodkowie

Sometimes American records just don't work out in the way that we want them to. Had I written this book ten years ago, this chapter would end with a meager statement in which I offer sincere hope that in one of those records, you will find the villages of origin for your ancestors. Thankfully we live in the age of the Internet. In the past few years, several projects have sprung up to index the church books of Poland. In addition to LDS, several other groups hope to make a complete index of Polish church book information a reality. The most important for the old settlers of Cook County Polonia is the Poznan Project.

Of the early Polish immigrants to Chicago, the majority came from the Prussian partition and, of them, the majority came from the Grand Duchy of Posen, the Polish province of Poznan or the state of Wielkopolski today. Rarely was a village recorded from these early immigrants when they were alive in the United States. Therefore, a genius named Lukasz Bielecki started a project to index all marriage records of that region of Poland so as to find the village of origin when the official documents only say that a person came from "Posen," "Prussia," or "Germany."

To use this website, find a married couple in your family tree. Perhaps it is your two direct ancestors or a collateral line. Even a distant relation will do. Just find two people who got married in Poland in the Prussian partition and punch their names into the Poznan Project's website: http://bindweed.man.poznan.pl/posen/search.php

This project has advanced rapidly through the years and covers much more than half of all marriages that took place in this region between 1835 and 1884. It has since expanded to include 1800 through 1899.

The website can be used in English and is extremely user-friendly. It also has a search feature that finds surnames similar (and relevant) to your query, unlike some other genealogical websites. Simply put, this is one of the best search engines I have used.

The search results reveal which church a couple married in (and, by extension, where they lived). In addition, Bielecki has a small page detailing what records still exist for that parish and whether they have been microfilmed. This website is an excellent resource for many of Chicago's Polonia, especially if they have early roots in the city.

Pomorze (http://www.ptg.gda.pl/index.php/certificate/action/searchM/) is a similar site, but it is more ambitious. This site indexes births, marriages, deaths, and other records of the northern Polish region of Pomerania for all years possible. Again, this is another excellent resource for those who have ancestry in far northern Poland. Many early settlers did come from West and East Prussia, so their information may be here.

Geneteka (http://www.geneteka.genealodzy.pl/index.php?op=se) is devoted simply to Poland, any city, any region. It contains indexes created by many volunteers but is scattered throughout time and space, unlike Poznan Project and Pomorze, which are more confined. It is likely an ancestor can be found here, but the information is so few and far between that finding an unknown ancestor here is like striking gold.

Przodkowie (http://www.przodkowie.com/metryki/en.php) was an attempt to index the church books mainly of the Russian partition of Poland similar to Bielecki's Poznan Project with the Prussian partition. The website seems to be defunct now with few new records being added to it recently. However, the existing data is still intact, and like Geneteka, there may be some wonderful results here.

As for these four websites, the Poznan Project is the best. That is why I volunteered to index records for this site. As much as I would love to index every church book that my ancestors were in, that is a feat that I alone probably could not accomplish in my lifetime. The Poznan Project is confined but in a good way. If you have ancestry in the Poznan region, then the odds are very, very good that you will find a marriage relating to your ancestors and consequently find their village of origin. Pomorze is an excellent site, and, with more data, may surpass Poznan Project in terms of its effectiveness for those of Pomeranian descent.

And of course, LDS is currently building an index of Polish records thanks to its army of volunteers. A few years from now, the LDS may have the greatest index. Currently, the records of the Lublin and Radom dioceses in Poland have indexing projects being completed by volunteers. Once that data becomes available, then it too will help to determine a village of origin.

LDS has published a baptism index for most localities in the Rzeszow diocese, so that may help if your ancestry is in southeastern Poland. This index will be most useful for those who have ancestry in the Ellis Island wave of immigrants from Galicia.

I urge you to join one of these sites and become a volunteer records indexer. For the four Polish records sites, all you have to do is order a roll of microfilm from LDS, record the information from it in the format that each respective site wants (usually an Excel spreadsheet), and then submit it to the webmaster to add to the site's database.

LDS is even easier; they provide the indexing program, images, and technical know-how. Simply register, download the program, pick the project you want to index, download a batch, and you are on your way to preserving history for future generations. All of these endeavors are grand and cannot be accomplished by one or two people; it takes many people to produce these working indexes. Therefore, I urge you to help with these efforts so that you and others can more easily find their ancestors and expand their family trees.

5. Naturalization Records

If your ancestor was naturalized after 1906, then the village of origin will be listed on the declaration of intent and the final papers. This will help with men naturalized between 1906 and the mid-1920s and then with both genders after that point because women had to be naturalized at the same time as their husbands.

Pre-1906 records will not list a village of origin. Also keep in mind that the village of origin may be different from the village of birth. My gg-grandmother's brother had "Brzesc Kujawski" listed as his birthplace on his naturalization record when in fact he was born in a village just outside of the town. Your ancestor may also simply have listed the big city or town close to where he or she was born instead of giving the actual village's name.

6. Social Security Applications

The odds of having a town listed along with country of origin on these records are excellent. If you are stuck, like I was, with an Austrian or Russian partition birth but no clue beyond that, try this route. These records are expensive but worth it if a village of origin is listed.

7. World War II Draft Card

Draft cards for men during World War II included a section for town and country of birth. Most people had something written there. Hopefully that can point you in the right direction. I only hope that this information is spelled correctly.

All of my ancestors had something written in for town. The information was not particularly helpful for my great-grandfather John Kruszka because "Volshv" does not exist in Poland (thankfully "Wieniec" does). However, that information is generally good and can help to locate your ancestral village on the map.

Some World War II draft cards included a village of birth, but the majority simply listed the partition of Poland and not the specific area.

8. Get Creative

Your relatives' ancestral origins can be elusive, but try to find as much as possible about them. Search through the PGSA's databases. Try to find employment records. Maybe they belonged to a club. If your ancestor belonged to the Osobnica Club of St. Peter and Paul Parish in Chicago, then he or she most likely originated in Osobnica, Poland. Do your best to recreate your relatives' life. Ask relatives for information. Search the Internet. Do whatever it takes. It can seem daunting, but it is necessary to find the village of origin before proceeding to the next step of research.

I Found the Village of Origin for My Ancestor. Now What?

Research that place of origin. In all seriousness, use Wikipedia for information. Wikipedia has a page for all Polish villages that exist today that links them with the *Gmina* (county) and region where a village is in Poland. Village names could be misspelled, so if Wikipedia turns up nothing, use a map website (e.g., Google Maps) that searches for villages with similar spellings.

If neither of those works, then it's time to go back to the olden days of genealogical research before the Internet by using maps and gazetteers. The local Family History Libraries operated by LDS in Naperville and Waukegan have historic maps of Poland that can assist in finding your village. It is possible that the village was wiped out in World War II, merged with a larger village, or simply was so small that everyone moved away and thus does not exist today.

Sifting through old maps and gazetteers is not a fun task. Thankfully, there is a web-based tool. It is an encyclopedia of the geography of Poland known as the *Slownik Geograficzny,* which was compiled in the late 1800s and early 1900s. Considering that is the time period of mass emigration from Poland, this resource will have the name of the village.

This book can be found online, and it has been digitized to allow for searching within the publication. Browsing the pages of it like a normal book is another way to use this resource. I recommend browsing if you cannot find your village by the above means. If it's not on Wikipedia, then it is possible that your village was "Wieniec" and not "Wenec" or "Wenich." Browsing the pages will help with that, not searching for those last two terms. Here is the website: http://dir.icm.edu.pl/pl/Slownik_geograficzny/

Even if you know the village of origin for your ancestor, then this is still an excellent resource to learn about the history of your village and what it was like when your ancestors left it (which is vastly different than today.) The resource is in Polish and contains many abbreviations and terms not commonly found today. The PGSA offers a translating service for entries in this book, but there is a long wait list attached to this service. I submitted my villages' entries to them years ago and still have yet to see them translated!

Another resource is Kartenmeister (http://www.kartenmeister.com/preview/databaseuwe.asp), which is a website dedicated to the Prussian partition of Poland along with other western lands in Poland that can help to find the village of origin with limited information such as a garbled village name on a poorly written vital record. This site is somewhat useful, but I have had greater success with the *Slownik*. However, the chance of finding another user of the site with ancestral roots in your village (and who has posted a message about it) is definitely worth a visit to this site.

CHAPTER TEN: POLISH LANGUAGE AND GENEALOGY

The Polish genealogy books that I have read have emphasized learning the Polish language to best research your ancestors. However, being able to read, write, or speak fluent Polish is not a prerequisite to engaging in Polish genealogy. Polish record keeping was so standardized that only a basic understanding of both Latin and Polish is needed to decipher the records of the Catholic Church and in other places.

Also remember that this is the Internet age. Simply look up any unfamiliar words online. An excellent resource of Polish genealogical words is on the LDS wiki: https://wiki.familysearch.org/en/Poland_Genealogical_Word_List And when in doubt, use Google Translate at www.google.com/translate.

The Polish alphabet uses the same letters as the English alphabet but with a few additions. The most important of these letters are ą (pronounced "an" or "am"), ę (pronounced like "en" or "em"), and ł (pronounced like "w"). Those letters may be confusing at first. Also keep in mind that j's are pronounced as y's in Polish, so the Polish surname Jablonski would actually be prounced with a Y at the beginning and not the J sound as in English. This can especially be seen in Polish records when first names are recorded. "Maciey" actually is "Maciej" and so on.

As far as Polish vocabulary, the best words to memorize are the months and numbers. Those are the most important, genealogically speaking, because they identify when a record was made and the ages of the people in them. Practice with these words, and they will begin to stick in your head.

Polish names are also important to know although they are similar to English and Latin names. Most English equivalents can easily be deduced by just looking at the name: Andrzej is Andrew, Jan is John, Elzbieta is Elizabeth, and so on. Some are rather difficult, such as Wojciech (Albert/Adalbert) and Wawrzyniec (Lawrence). Never fear! The PGSA translation guide has a section on Polish names and their English equivalents (along with several other useful categories of translations) right here: http://www.pgsa.org/PDFs/DzChicObit.pdf

Do not let a foreign language intimidate you. Learn the basics. Give it a try. Keep at it, and you will accomplish your task. The difficult part will be finding your ancestors' records, not reading them.

CHAPTER ELEVEN: POLISH CHURCH AND VITAL RECORDS

It is now time to continue your research backward in time using Polish records. Establish the lines of your family tree using Polish church records and then hopefully supplement that information using other types of records such as census records, military records, and land records.

Of course, when it comes to records and record accessibility, Poland and the United States are about as different as countries can be. There is no Polish version of the Freedom of Information Act (FOIA), so Polish archives are not obligated to show anything. What they do provide can cost quite a bit of money for them to photocopy and mail or scan to you. Therefore, I recommend the LDS route of research before attempting to contact an archive in Poland.

The most economical route for Polish genealogy is to order microfilms of church records from LDS rather than writing to a Polish archives asking for photocopies of their records. LDS has microfilmed millions of Polish church records, and they are all readily available to order. Search for your ancestors' village of origin on www.familysearch.org under "catalog" and either "place" or "keyword." The search results will then display the types of records that LDS has microfilmed.

Typically, LDS only has church records for small villages but will have land and other records for larger settlements. It's the luck of the draw when it comes to these records; some villages have intact records dating back to the early 1600s. Others have been destroyed completely before World War II era. It's part of the accident of birth; were you born to people whose ancestral villages' records are still intact?

Order the rolls of microfilm for your village from the LDS central archives in Salt Lake City, Utah. This is an easy process that can be done one of two ways. The first way is to go into your local family history center, ask for an order form, and fill out the film number for that roll of microfilm. If you live in the Chicagoland area, visit either the Naperville or Waukegan libraries. Both of those locations have many Chicago records and rolls of microfilm with Polish records on them. Find a family history library near your home with this tool: https://www.familysearch.org/locations. The library staff can help further with finding the correct film and ordering it if necessary.

The second way is to order the film online. The Naperville location does not fill out written film requests anymore and will direct you to the computer when you ask them to order a film for you. Films can be ordered from here: https://www.familysearch.org/films/. Online ordering can be done for LDS libraries in most parts of the United States and many parts of the world. Simply follow the instructions onscreen and be sure to establish which library you want the film to be sent to.

It can take anywhere from two weeks to six months for the film to arrive, but it is worth the wait. On average it will take three weeks, but I know of many people who have waited months and months for a film to arrive. Once it arrives, search for your immigrant ancestor. Once you have found his or her marriage or baptism record, then you have just begun the next step of Polish genealogy—tracing your family back to its origins in Poland!

Polish recordkeeping can be divided based on the partitions that Poland suffered in the late 1700s. I highly recommend reading a history of Poland because it helps to gain a new appreciation of what our ancestors went through in the Old World.

This chapter is broken into three parts to cover the three parts of Poland and the different styles of record-keeping that churches used in the three partitions. They are in order from easiest to research to hardest, in my personal opinion. Granted, each location has its own benefits/challenges, but in general, this order holds true for the second to fifth-generation American genealogist. Each section is divided into relative time frames for each format of record-keeping.

1. Records From 966 to 1562

Few records were kept during the early days of Poland's history. The only way to find an ancestor during this time period was if he or she was a member of the upper nobility (the magnates), royalty, or was noteworthy in some way such as being the president of a university (and therefore probably was upper nobility if selected for that position). Do not be too disappointed. This is on par with genealogy in virtually all parts of Europe. Record-keeping for the masses was not done in full scale until the 1600s or 1700s for most regions of Europe.

Also, few people in Poland had surnames at this point, so even if records existed for peasant lineages, it would be impossible to prove who exactly your ancestor was. This type of research is best left for the advanced researcher who already has a well-produced family tree, is fluent in modern and old Polish, and has easy access to many different archives in Poland.

2. Pre-Partition Records From 1563 to 1773

Finding records from this time period is difficult but not impossible. The Catholic Church, in the Council of Trent, mandated that all births and marriages had to be recorded from 1563 onward. It later issued a separate decree that deaths had to also be recorded. Different regions of Poland caught on to this at different times, but by the 1600s, all localities recorded births, marriages, and deaths. The oldest church records in Poland can be found in its big towns and cities, such as Krakow and Poznan, but do exist for a few lucky communities around Poland.

Sadly, the majority of these records have been lost to the ages for many reasons. Many people believe that they were destroyed in World War II. Although it is true that many records were destroyed in Poland's many wars, other factors often overlooked are Poland's climate and the physical nature of these records. Churches were usually just wooden structures; stone was not a common building material in rural Poland until much later. These books were written on plain paper, not vellum or anything more durable. Through the years, floods, fires, and other acts of nature destroyed more records than an army ever could.

Another thing to keep in mind is whether these records are legible. I have gotten my hopes up by looking at rolls of microfilm from the 1600s only to be dismayed at how worn the records were. Sometimes the words have faded away. Sometimes the paper is in pieces. Sometimes the handwriting is just plain mystifying.

And yet another obstacle to these records is that surnames were not common in Poland during this time period either. By this time, the nobility had fixed surnames, but the surnames of the peasants still tended to be fluid. Towns were small and life expectancy was short; the priest knew everyone, so why should he record any more than he had to?

Even those with surnames may have changed them over the years. In the Austrian partition, I have an ancestral line known as Swieton in a marriage record from the 1770s but is known as Jelen from the 1780s onward. Surnames were not considered permanent legacies until the late 1700s and they could have been fluid even then.

Probably the most frustrating moment of my genealogical search is when I saw on several films from several different locations that the surnames of godparents were recorded on eighteenth-century baptismal records, but neither the surname of the child nor the father or the mother was recorded.

I am not saying this to discourage you but to instead brace yourself for what could happen and know that you are not alone in your frustration. We as Poles have a lot stacked against us, but this genealogical search is possible; it just takes time, determination, and a bit of luck.

3. Austrian Partition—Southeastern Poland

This is the region known as Galicia in southeastern Poland, and it is where I got my start in Polish genealogy. The region was the poorest in Poland with the greatest disparity between the rich and poor and the lowest amount of social mobility. It is no wonder then that Galician immigrants made up the greatest percentage of Polish immigrants in the history of Polish immigration to the United States.

The Austrian partition was a rather medieval society. There was little movement among villages, and the people there were still serfs *de facto* even though serfdom had been abolished *de jur* when Poland was first partitioned in the 1790s in this region. This sounds horrible, but it actually makes genealogy that much easier. My Prussian partition ancestors bounced from parish to parish as they moved around in search of employment; my Austrian partition ancestors are all found in the same parish with only one exception.

Austrian partition records are the easiest records for a native English speaker to read. I did not understand any Polish when I first got started, and I learned this style of record-keeping the fastest. These records were kept in Latin in a columnar format that had been imposed upon the church by its Austrian overlords. I applaud the conquerors for this; this format kept beautiful, informative records that make research in this region easy (relatively speaking).

Records From 1563 to 1788

Church records from this partition at this time have little information. However, beggars can't be choosers. They were kept in Latin and reflect the style typically seen throughout pre-partition Poland. A typical baptism entry from this time lists the first name of the father and mother along with their child. It lists the day, month, and year of birth along with the full names of the two godparents. Usually a surname will be given to the father in the record but not always. The father's occupation may be listed or it could simply indicate that he was a peasant or farmer. A marriage record will include the full name of the bride and groom, their wedding date, and the witnesses. Death records were the least detailed, usually recording only the first name of the deceased along with date of burial. It may give an age at death. However, it should list if it was a child, *infantem*, and then may list the name of the father of the child. This style may be difficult to obtain and read. However, finding these records will push your family tree back further than most Polish-Americans' trees.

The rule of genealogy is to start with the present and work backward. This strategy works well for this time period. Start with your nineteenth-century ancestors and establish their lineages using birth, marriage, and death records. Then search for the names of their parents in the death records of the later period to get an idea of how old they were when they died. This has helped me with finding records for my gggggg-grandfather Paul Kliszor/Kleszynski. He died in Szczawnica, Galicia, in 1817 at the age of 56, so I was able to search for his birth record starting in the early 1760s. A caveat with this rule is that the ages recorded on death records usually were off by as much as five to ten years. These ages should give a general idea but are not always an absolute fact.

It is difficult establishing lineages from these early records, but it can be done. Be patient, thoroughly read the records, and do your best. It may be easiest to start an indexing project and then submit your data to Geneteka. That way, each entry in that church book was covered in the search for a trace of your ancestors.

Records From 1789 to 1918

Although the Austrian partition actually happened in 1773, it took a while for the Austrian mode of record-keeping to take effect. A variety of this style was kept in some parishes from 1776 onward, but in most localities, the changeover happened between 1788 and 1792. That's the time to note because that is when record-keeping became serious business. Austria mandated that all people, including Jews, Greek Orthodox, and others, had to be recorded in the church books of the Catholic Church because these books were used for conscription purposes.

The Austrian military was always in need of soldiers, and Austria conscripted many Poles into service using these books. The leaders of the draft could ascertain the number of men of military age in a town simply by glancing through these church books to see who had been born roughly eighteen to twenty-five years previously. This is why these records were so meticulously kept.

The amount of information found on a record increases as time passes, so it is wise to collect information about all of the siblings of your ancestors because the youngest sibling probably has the most information on his or her baptism entry compared to the first- or second-born child. The first child of my gggg-grandfather Jacob Gabrys was born in Szczawnica in 1823. His last child was born in 1866 (he was married twice). The record from 1866 tells far more about him than the 1823 record does.

Baptism entries had the date of birth, date of baptism, house number, name of child, full name of father, name of mother, mother's maiden name, first name of mother's father, two godparents, and then all of their respective statuses in society. These records have wonderful information, and they are organized easily in columns that give all of this information. Yes, these records are in Latin, but the columns make it easy to find information. The best part is that the later records have even more information on them; the grandparents of the child are added in the second half of the nineteenth century for both the paternal and maternal sides of the family.

Keep in mind that godparents were deliberately chosen by the parents because they were expected to help raise the child and nurture them spiritually and physically. Therefore, there may be a blood link between the godparents and a child, or those godparents may have been good friends or neighbors of your ancestors. One way to determine the status of your ancestor in the town he or she lived was to see how often he or she was chosen as a godparent. If your ancestors were picked a lot, then they were popular and well-liked people.

Marriage entries had the date of marriage, house number of the groom and bride, their ages, their full names, either the full name of each of their fathers or the full name of each of their parents, and the names of the witnesses to the marriage.

In contrast to godparents, marriage witnesses were simply people who were around that day who were willing to watch the ceremony and could be called on later on in case something happened to the original record to testify that the marriage actually happened. There could have been a special connection between the witnesses and those getting married, but there didn't have to be.

Death entries are the least detailed but are easy to sift through. These included the name of the decedent, their place in society (were they an infant? the wife of somebody? the widow of somebody?) date of death, date of burial, house number, and some kind of cause of death. The cause of death typically was not detailed. Often the priest only wrote that it was a "natural death" or the person died of "old age," but if there was something unusual about the death, then it was recorded. Dying by unnatural means was extremely rare in Poland in this time. Violent crimes and murder (outside of wartime) were unheard of in the rural Polish countryside. The odds of finding an unnatural death are much greater in Cook County than in any rural county in Poland in this era.

Numerus Domus

One element that all of these records have in common is the house number, the *numerus domus*. This is the defining feature of Austrian-partition records and is one of the greatest tools in your genealogical toolkit. The house number was like an old-fashioned address for this family. A house number was the number assigned to a home that applied to everyone living in it, whether he was the man who built the house or the infant daughter whose parents stayed there because their own home was destroyed in a big storm.

From early records in this partition, it can be difficult to establish firm familial relationships especially if your ancestor was a Marianna, wife of John Nowak (a common name). House numbers are a way around that. If there is a Marianna Nowak in death entries with the same house number as the Marianna Nowak who gave birth to your ancestor, then the odds are good that it is her in that entry.

House numbers alone cannot prove anything, but they can help prove certain things and establish firmer relationships. Also, keep in mind that in this time, extended families often lived together. Just because someone has the same surname as your ancestor and the same house number, do not assume that they are siblings. They could be cousins. They could be uncle/nephew or aunt/niece. They could even just be friends with the same surname.

There are also some parishes in the southern part of the Russian partition, near the Austrian partition's border, that recorded a house number. Keep this in mind when you are researching the Russian partition as well as the Austrian partition.

I highly recommend keeping track of all those listed at the house number of your ancestors because it can help down the line. Also, making a list of the different house numbers of your ancestors over time is useful because house numbers changed once every fifty years or so in a village.

Conclusion

Austrian partition records are the easiest Polish church records to sift through, so start with them. These records are legible and in a standard columnar format with information for the full duration after a church's institution. There is no changing back and forth between formats. There is no changing back and forth between languages even. All of these records are in columns, in Latin, and contain good information that can easily expand your family tree backward in time.

4. Prussian Partition/Prussian States—Northwestern and Western Poland

I will do my best to summarize Prussian church records, but the word that I hesitate using is "summarize." Of the three partitions, the Germanic/Prussian regions of Poland had the greatest variance in the styles of record-keeping. There are two basic methods of record-keeping that churches used, but when each style was used varied from church to church. The information recorded varied in how the pages were set up.

Therefore, it is necessary to discuss styles of record-keeping rather than eras of record-keeping as done with the Austrian partition. One thing that makes the Prussian partition unique is that the pre-partition style of record-keeping held on past the partitioning era, in some cases all the way down to the 1840s. That is not a good thing for genealogists because those have little information on them compared to the other styles. Many Prussian records are in Latin, but there are many in Polish and some in German.

Paragraph Style – late 1500s to the mid 1800s

The paragraph style of record-keeping was used from the late 1500s until the mid-1800s in the Prussian partition with the amount of information given in the paragraph gradually increasing as the years passed. Generally speaking, each record is a block of text with the village name given on the side. Don't let that distract though; peasant families often moved from village to village in search of work so don't search only for a particular village. Search the records of the whole parish.

Baptism records in this style give the child's name, father's full name, father's status in town, mother's name and maiden name, godparents' names, date of birth, and sometimes hour of birth.

Marriage records give the full name of the groom and bride, their ages, which village they came from, and the witnesses' names. Their parents' names may have been recorded, but they probably were not in this style of record-keeping.

Death records with this style are decent. They gave the full name of the decedent including the maiden name if the woman who died was married. The date of death was usually given, but always given was the date of burial, which was a day or two after the day of death. Later records give a cause of death, but they usually just recorded that the death was of natural causes. If it was an infant who died, the names of the parents were provided in the form of "John and Mary Nowakow" (the married couple John and Mary Nowak.)

This style can be found from early records down to the 1800s. These are solid records that can help build your family tree. They do not give much detail, but they give the basic facts. The major drawback to this style is that it takes a long time to locate the key information inside paragraph after paragraph while searching for your ancestors. This is the most time consuming of the Prussian record-keeping styles.

Columnar Style

Some time in the 1800s, the parish in the Prussian partition would have adopted a more Germanic style of record-keeping that is detailed, efficient, and makes sense. In other words, it was quite German. The church began keeping records in a column format that is similar to the Austrian partition and continued using this style all the way down to the twentieth century. These records are faster to flip through and easily display the information needed without needing to read all of the text as before.

The difference between this columnar style and that of Austria is that Austria's column style was done in a standard format using the same form throughout the history of the parishes there. These Prussian parishes tended to mix it up as the years went by, using different forms and headings. This style can be loaded with information or can be rather plain. Hope that it was a young, competent priest with clear handwriting who serviced your ancestors. This style was used in the Prussian partition starting in the 1820s for some parishes but wasn't fully adopted in the region until the 1860s.

The following information was recorded on the best baptism records with this style: the child's name, date of birth, date of baptism, village of birth, hour of birth, father's full name, father's religion, father's profession, mother's name plus maiden name, mother's religion, and the godparents' names, status, and religion. With the columnar format, most of this information is in clean, easy-to-scan columns.

Marriage records are good for the most part, but some can be frustrating. Marriage records list the groom's full name, the bride's full and maiden names, their ages, their marital status (single, widowed, or *deflorata* ,which means an unmarried woman who has had sex before), their villages of origin, and the witnesses. Usually their parents' names are given but not always.

Death records with this style are wonderful and are the best of all the three partitions because they give the most information. On a typical death record, the person's name will be given along with the name of his or her spouse. Women's maiden names are given. If it was a child who died, then the names of the parents will be given. Sometimes parents' names are recorded even if the person was not a child. A day of death, day of burial, cause of death, village of death, and sometimes time of death are given. The best part is that usually when a person was married or widowed when they died; it lists how many of their children are alive.

I was lucky to find on my ggg-grandfather's death record the names of all of his children including his daughters' married names. This information is given on the far right side of the death record. The key word is "*liberi*" which tells how many living children that person had. The cause of death is usually specific, and the person's status will be recorded.

Other Styles

The parishes of the Prussian partition tended to bounce between record-keeping formats. One parish that I researched extensively used paragraph format in the early 1800s, columnar format in the 1820s, paragraph format in the 1830s and 1840s, and then back again to columns in the 1850s onward. No matter what format your parish used, simply look for the key pieces of information.

Getting a good Latin-to-English translation guide is nice but is not necessary. Most Latin is self-explanatory (*nomine* is name, *aetus* is age, etc.). I purchased a Latin-to-English dictionary and was disappointed because classic, textbook Latin is not used in Polish recordkeeping. This is church Latin that has been adapted to fit the records. For example, the term for an unmarried male is *juvenus*. There is no letter J in classic Latin. Printing a copy of the LDS Latin-to-English guide or another site's genealogical Latin guide is the best way to read these records.

Don't let the changing formats intimidate you. Prussian records are well written and contain excellent information. I'd recommend researching Prussian ancestry after having worked a while with your Austrian ancestry. Another thing to keep in mind is that the parishes of this partition were bigger than in Austria and weren't as self-contained. This means that they typically extend onto more rolls of microfilm than the Austrian partition's parishes. That means more records to look through and more films to order.

Another monkey wrench in the Prussian genealogy search is that during the Napoleonic Wars, certain parts of the Prussian partition adopted the Napoleonic code of record-keeping. My ancestral parish of Trzemeszno kept all of its records in this format from 1808 to 1809, the years of greatest hope for Poland in its partitioning period; this is the period the Polish national anthem mentions. The Napoleonic code is the standard of record-keeping in the Russian partition from 1808 onward, so let's move on to the next section.

5. Russian Partition—Eastern Poland

For native Poles, this will be the easiest area to research. However, this book is primarily about American genealogy and is intended for an English-speaking audience. The records of this region were kept in the vernacular, Polish. This would not be a problem if the columnar style was used rather than the Napoleonic code, which was used for more than one hundred years in this region. Learning about Napoleon's system of record-keeping is a must before attempting to research this partition's records.

Before 1808, Russian partition records were similar to those of the other regions before columnar style was introduced. They were written in Latin and contained the same information as the other partitions. They were not detailed; they were short and to the point in paragraph format. If the locality was located close to Galicia, then it may have used the Austrian format of record-keeping from the 1770s until the 1800s. Check an old map of the region to see whether this would be the case for your village of origin.

However, all of this changed with the Congress Kingdom of Poland and the Duchy of Warsaw. Without getting into a big history lesson here, this region of Poland was set up as its own autonomous body when Napoleon invaded and freed the inhabitants from the clutches of Russia. Napoleon formed the Duchy of Warsaw, which later evolved into the Congress Kingdom. Both of these systems failed when Napoleon failed, but the French style of keeping records persisted throughout the ages. This is a detailed system of record-keeping that tells a lot about your ancestors from this region. However, if you are not fluent in Polish, then learning this style will take more time and effort than the other partitions did.

The first step toward tackling these records is to understand what the Napoleonic Code is and what kind of information can be found in the different records. LDS has an excellent guide to these types of records here: https://wiki.familysearch.org/en/Poland_Civil_Registration-_Vital_Records#Format_of_a_Napoleonic_Birth_Record_in_Polish

Do not attempt to study these records before learning about the format they are in because they are unlike anything else in the United States or Poland.

The long style of the Napoleonic Code was used from its inception in 1808 until the mid-1820s when the short style was adopted. Do not worry; no genealogical information was sacrificed in this changeover, only the legalese that is of no use to genealogists was shortened. Those early records had poorer handwriting and more words to read, so they take longer to go through than the shorter records.

The amount of information found in these records is staggering. In baptism records, the name of the child, parents' full names, parents' ages, father's occupation, dates of birth and baptism, hour of birth, village of birth, and information about the witnesses was all recorded. The key difference between these records and those of the other partitions is that the parents' ages are recorded as well. This information is not recorded in the other partitions and is helpful when trying to find their marriage record and respective baptism records.

Marriage records too have a wonderful amount of information. They list the full names of the bride and groom, their ages, society status, parents' full names, date of marriage, the villages each came from, the days that the banns were read, whether the couple made a prenuptial agreement, and information about the witnesses. It also says whether the bride and groom's parents are still alive, which is useful when trying to find their death records. Marriage records are typically the most detailed and may contain even more information beyond the ordinary; my gg-grandfather's marriage record recorded information about his military service in the Russian army.

Death records from this region can be disappointing. Because of all that wonderful information given in birth and marriage records, I assumed that death records would be equally as informative. Death records simply state the full name of the deceased, name of his or her spouse, age of death, village of death, and witnesses to the dead body. Some records give the names of the deceased's parents if the deceased is an adult. If the deceased is a child, the parents' names will always be given. No cause of death was recorded unless it was something out of the ordinary. These records are still good but are disappointing in comparison to the other vital records.

Indices

One special and redeeming feature of the Napoleonic code of record-keeping is that after every year, these records were probably indexed. In other words, there should be an index at the end of each year for each birth/marriage/death section that lists the names of the people found in that section in alphabetical order along with the page number and entry number of that record.

These indices will help in the search considerably. Again, transcribed information is no substitute for the original and sometimes priests skipped over records in the indices, so full-scale searching may very well have to take place with these records. However, finding an ancestor's name in an index saves considerable time and effort.

Indices are not exclusive to the Russian partition; some larger parishes from West Prussia and other regions indexed records by year. In fact, I know of one parish from that region had a master index of all records from the 1600s and 1700s that was created in the early 1800s. However, indices are standard in the Russian partition and not finding an index of records would be the exception to the rule in this region.

Records in Russian

There is one bad snag when researching this partition. Another short history lesson is needed here. In 1863 the remaining nobility and intellects of Poland led an uprising against their Russian overlords with the peasants backing them up. Unfortunately, this uprising failed, and the Poles were punished for their insubordination. One such punishment was that their language was stripped away in all official records. The only language that could be used in record-keeping was the official language of the Russian Empire, Russian. This became the law beginning in 1868, which means that all official church records are in Russian after this year, not Polish.

Now don't despair. The Poles living in that time were no happier about this decree than you are now. Those brave priests fought back in small ways. Some parishes recorded the official records in Russian, but some continued to write duplicates in Polish as did my ancestral parish in Wieniec, Wloclawek. Most parishes would record the person's name in Polish and Russian at this time, so it is still possible to determine who is who in the records. It just takes more time than with the other partitions.

All that being said, Russian is a language similar to Polish but so very different from English. Russian uses the Cyrillic alphabet, not the Latin alphabet as both English and Polish do. Keep in mind also that these records were written in cursive handwriting, so running some names and phrases through Google Translate does not produce the style of letters that are seen on these documents.

If you can't read Russian, then these records will be difficult to decipher. Get help to read these because you do not want to make a mistake with the information found in the record. Talk to the staff at a nearby LDS family history library to see if a staff member or patron can read Russian and would be willing to help. A translation guide is helpful and practical for the Polish records, but it is nearly unusable for the Russian records simply because of the nature of the language and the style of the records.

These records are rich, detailed, and filled with wonderful genealogical information. These are the most difficult records for the American genealogist to search, but it can be done. Find a translation guide for the Polish records. Learn some basic Polish words, and you will be able to crack these records.

CHAPTER TWELVE: POLISH RESEARCH AND BEYOND

Beyond church books, using Polish records in the United States can be difficult. LDS has microfilmed other types of Polish records, but the coverage is spotty. The larger the population of your ancestral town, the more likely there is to be more records beyond church records still in existence, let alone microfilmed and available for genealogists to use. Civil registries exist for the Prussian partition after secular civil registration was instituted in 1874, but few of these records were microfilmed. Most are scattered in the archives across what was the Prussian partition with some Lutheran records being kept at the central archives in Berlin. Land records exist for some localities but not all. Some census records exist for certain parts of Poland, but again, few of these records have been microfilmed.

There is a plethora of resources to research Polish family history. The sad thing is that many records can only be accessed in Poland. Writing letters to archives and having their staff do genealogical searches can get costly. Then again, making a trip to Poland can be costly, too. In other words, once the resources of church books have been exhausted, then you have just about reached the genealogical end, so to speak.

Once you are at this point, no tell-all book will give the answers. It is up to you to see what other records are around. All genealogists need to make a trip back to their homeland at some point. Go with a genealogical tourism company that can help you visit your ancestral villages as well as help you find living relatives and documents in the archives. At the minimum, travel with a guide who can provide translation and genealogical assistance for you. The PGSA can help with planning these kinds of trips

Military Records in Poland

The odds are good that some of your ancestors served in the armed forces of one of the partitioning powers. It is possible that your ancestors served in the old Polish army, but the probability of that is less because military duty was mostly confined to the ranks of the nobility. The odds are low if your ancestors were serfs because the lords did not want their serfs trained in combat.

The records of the Prussian military were virtually all destroyed in World War II. The only records that remain are those of military officers, the German nobility, so they probably won't be of much use to the Polish. I'm sorry to say that this type of research can't be done for Prussia.

The records of the Russian partition exist but are locked away in Russian archives. I have never done this type of research, and you will be hard pressed to find a genealogist who has. Knowledge of the Russian language is critical to begin this type of research, so contact the archives of the area of Poland where your ancestors came from and ask them where Russian military records from that region are held. The rest is up to you. Best of luck because you will need it to find the correct archives and navigate the Russian bureaucracy to get at those records.

Now, the records of the Austrian partition, mainly Galicia, are extant and many have been microfilmed by LDS. However, these records have not been indexed in any way, shape, or form. It will require sifting through dozens of rolls of microfilm to find information about your ancestor. The prerequisite to doing that is determining which military recruitment district he or she lived in. That information can be found on this map: http://upload.wikimedia.org/wikipedia/commons/9/9d/Corps_of_Austria-Hungary.jpg

Search for your Galician town on this map, and find the military district that your ancestor lived in. That was the easy part. The hard part is sifting through all the paperwork of that region to find a glimpse of your ancestor. Sometimes if a man served in the armed forces in this region, it was noted on his baptismal record.

Another clue to military service was the age your male ancestor was married. If he was conscripted into the military, then he would not have been able to get married until after he was discharged, which typically happened when he was between the ages of 25 and 29. If a man waited to get married until that time in Galicia, then often that meant he was in the military. Non-military men got married around the age of 20 or 21. Galician military records can be found, but it will take a great deal of time, patience, and good command of the German language.

Other Records: Land and Census Records

All areas in Poland have been subjected to censuses of population, land, capital, and more during the course of their history. The big question is whether those records survived. Sadly, the only answer that I can give for that is that it is the accident of your ancestors' birth. Were your ancestors born in a village whose records are intact?

Censuses were taken many times during the era of partitions in Poland, but few returns that include personal information about the people survive. Most were destroyed. A list of censuses done by the partitioning powers can be found by doing an Internet search of the name of the partitioning power with the words "census" and "historic."

Some land census records survive in archives in Poland, but again, few have been microfilmed and thus require research in that archives in Poland. At this point, all that can be done is to go to Poland (or hire someone who lives there), visit the depository that holds the original documents for your village of origin, and hope for the best. The rest is up to fate.

Polish research can be done outside of Poland, but it is more difficult. Beyond church books, researching Polish ancestors is difficult. If you can afford it, hire a professional to perform other types of records searches within Polish archives.

Finding a reputable professional is a great task, too. Consult the PGSA or another Polish genealogical organization for tips on who is reputable and how he or she can be reached. All that being said, it is well worth the effort. Give it your all to find those ancestors!

CHAPTER THIRTEEN: DNA AND GENETIC GENEALOGY

An area of genealogy in which Poles are under-represented is the realm of genetic genealogy. DNA is a fantastic new way to uncover new family members and missing branches of your family tree, and many genealogists of other ethnicities have whole-heartedly embraced it. However, on the major genetic genealogy sites, there are few Polish-American researchers.

A. What Is It?

Genetic genealogy is genealogy based up the scientific study of a person's DNA compared against both large populations' DNA markers and the DNA markers of other individuals.

DNA is the material of inheritance. It is the stuff, so to speak, that gets passed down from parents to children that contains the instructions for how to build a human being. Of course, all human beings are different, thus so is their DNA; no two human beings have the exact same strand of DNA short of identical twins. They have the same DNA because they formed after a single fertilized egg split into two early in the gestation process; thus each half has the same genetic material.

Aside from identical twins, every other human being has a distinct strand of DNA because of the nature of sexual reproduction. When a human being creates sperm or egg, the body splits its DNA into infinite combinations to fill up all of those sex cells. That is what produces the variations seen in the world today.

We as genealogists can use that variation to try to find long-lost relatives. Scientists can decode those variances into a long string of letters based on the base pairs that make up a strand of DNA. Once a strand of DNA has been sequenced, then it can be studied to see how it compares against other peoples' DNA strands.

The first step to doing this is to purchase a home DNA testing kit from a company that performs ancestral DNA testing. That company will send a kit with all the necessary materials. You swab the inside of your cheek or provide saliva in a small vial, and then mail it back to the company where they will break apart your cells to get at the DNA and then sequence it.

In other words, they will read your DNA and then use it to determine ancestry, medical traits, or anything else that they test for in a person's DNA. While I highly recommend doing a DNA test for medical reasons to see your susceptibility to diseases and the strength of the systems of your body, I will only cover the genealogical reasons here.

B. How Does DNA Testing Impact the Field of Genealogy? How Would It Help Me?

DNA testing is no substitute for the traditional genealogical research covered in this book. In fact, without the traditional paper trail, there is little hope of getting much out of DNA testing. Without a family tree stretching back as far as it possibly can, then the odds of finding a relative via DNA are slim.

Relatives can be found one of three ways, and of those methods, the third is the most likely. Once your DNA has been sequenced, three tools can be used to determine ancestry, if you are a man.

Sadly, if you are a woman, there are only two. For men, the first way to determine ancestry is via your Y chromosome. The Y chromosome determines the male gender and thus can only be passed from father to son and so on. That Y chromosome can be placed into a group based on which specific genetic markers it has on it.

These specific markers are called mutations. As DNA replicates over the years, it can also change because of the nature of DNA replication. These accumulated changes over time are what cause evolution as well as the variety seen in living creatures today. Group placement is determined by which mutations are present in your strand of DNA.

The groups that people are placed in are called haplogroups and are used to determine meta-ancestry. They can tell which general region of the world your direct male ancestor came from. If there is an individual on the website who matches all of the mutations on your Y chromosome, then he very well could be a relative that shares your direct male line. This is rare but can be done. This type of ancestral research is more fun than useful. It can be done to determine meta-ancestry such as a Native American Y chromosome being found in someone whose ancestors have been here since colonial times or a Viking Y chromosome in someone from Scotland. This probably won't help build more branches in your family tree, but it is fun to know.

R1 is the haplogroup of the Indo-Europeans who migrated (or conquered, depending on who is talking about it) from the Middle East to Europe ten thousand years ago. More than 90 percent of European men have this haplogroup. It can then be divided into two groups: R1a for Eastern Europeans and R1b for Western Europeans. There are other haplogroups that white Europeans could belong to, but these two are the most common in Europeans today.

As for Polish–Americans, the most likely Y chromosome haplogroup is R1a1. This is the haplogroup of the western Slavs and happens to be my haplogroup. R1b is found among the Poles who have a more western direct male ancestor such as an ancient Celt from Germany rather than a Slav from the east. More information about a specific haplogroup can be found on the website of the company with whom you test. Also, searching for that haplogroup on Google yields some good resources about it.

The second route to discovering ancestry through DNA can be done for both men and women and involves the mitochondrial DNA (mtDNA) of the cells that make up the body. The mitochondria are the things inside of your body's cells that provide energy. The mitochondria have their own DNA strand, separate from that of the rest of your body. This is beautiful, because mtDNA is transmitted from mother to daughter or son. Men cannot pass mtDNA to their offspring, except for a one in three billion chance, so studying mtDNA is like studying the ancestry of your mother's mother's mother and so on. Therefore, sequencing the mtDNA will determine ancestry on your direct maternal line.

Finding an ancestor via this route is more difficult than any other method and is nearly impossible. For two living people to find each other via this method, they would need to have every single marker in common and a well-developed family tree stretching back at least two hundred years. mtDNA mutates at a slower rate than normal DNA, which means that even two people with identical mtDNA strands do not have to have an ancestor in the recent past; they could have shared an ancestor two hundred years ago or one thousand years ago.

But again, mtDNA haplogroup research is more about having fun than actually finding something or someone quantifiable. These haplogroups are different than Y chromosome haplogroups; do not get confused between the two. It is more difficult to discuss mtDNA haplogroups in Polish ancestry because there are many more possibilities. The most common haplogroup in European populations, as well as in Poland, is H. There are many different subclades of that haplogroup, so it is best to do your own research about your particular haplogroup. My haplogroup is X2C1, a mysterious group that less than 2 percent of Europeans, and fewer Poles, belong to. I can't explain it and of course my maternal line is the one where I have hit the brick wall. Typical.

The third method of using DNA for genealogical purposes is via the autosomal DNA route. Aside from the mtDNA and the Y chromosome, genealogists can use some specific markers on the rest of their DNA to discover ancestry. Some sites offer a method of finding living relatives using this route. This is the one most likely to produce results. The funny thing about DNA is that only certain parts of it get passed on; after all, we are not clones of our parents. We are unique humans produced from different parts of our parents. That is how children of the same parents have varying hair colors and eye colors.

Therefore, certain markers get passed on whereas others die out. Relatives are found by searching for segments on your chromosomes that you and another person have in common.

C. What Company Should I Use to Test My DNA?

Genealogists should continue their work with a company that is friendly toward them and offers resources for continuing their family trees. Therefore, I recommend using one of two websites to test your DNA: www.familytreedna.com or www.23andme.com

In my opinion, 23andme is the best company to use. It is cheaper than Family Tree DNA, tests medical traits as well as ancestry, and has more useful applications than Family Tree DNA.

Both sites offer a relative-finder application that sequences your autosomal DNA, and the company works its magic to try to match those sequences with other people who have gotten their DNA tested. A results screen along with a probability reading of how likely it is you are related to that person will show what happened.

Remember, not all autosomal DNA is passed on, and it can play tricks. Y chromosome and mtDNA inheritance is understood much better than autosomal inheritance. Just because you share a segment of your DNA does not mean that you are instant cousins. It just means you shared an ancestor some time in the past, be it 100 years ago or 1000 years ago. There is a popular theory that states that all Europeans are descended from a person who lived 3000 years ago; that does not produce much confidence on our part.

Therefore, the best way to do this type of research is to use the relative-finder application as a guide. If 23andme or Family Tree DNA says that this person may be your fourth cousin, then contact him or her. Ask him or her about their family tree and then compare yours to theirs. If there is an apparent connection, then that is spectacular.

If not, continue work on your family tree and urge the other person to do the same. DNA can open doors for genealogists when used properly.

Both of these are reputable sites committed to helping people discover their ancestry. If I had to choose, I would choose 23andme because I see it as the wave of the future as opposed to Family Tree DNA, which has had its time and seems to be fading away. However, both are great resources.

Another company is www.dnatribes.com, where I also had my DNA tested. This site has a different philosophy than others described in this chapter. It sequences various parts of your autosomal DNA and then determines your ancestral "tribe." It breaks down your DNA, analyzes it in comparison to large groups of DNA data known as populations from different countries of origin, and then determines whether you have any ancestry in that country. It's a fun way to look at your ancestry, but it really cannot help in your genealogical search.

D. Conclusion

When I speak to ordinary people about DNA testing for ancestry, they get excited. When I speak to genealogists about DNA testing for ancestry, they get skeptical. I urge all genealogists to get their DNA tested. Will they break through that brick wall and discover long lost cousins as some companies advertise? Maybe, but probably not. The only way to find out is to give it a try. The technology is advancing at such a rapid rate that new discoveries are made with each passing day. We as genealogists would be fools not to take advantage of a tool that has the potential to connect long lost cousins.

Granted, it is rather expensive. And it is kind of scary for some people that these strangers can tell so much just from a little bit of saliva. 23andme gives the option for them to keep your DNA on file in their laboratory or to destroy the sample once they have completed testing it. I recommend keeping your DNA on file, because if a new testing method comes out, then the sample will be there, and you won't have to re-submit a sample. It is perfectly safe to do so; they are not making clones or splicing your genes into monkeys or anything ridiculous like that. The people at 23andme and Family Tree DNA are committed to helping people discover ancestry through DNA, and that is what their respective companies stand for.

I want to see more Polish–Americans getting their DNA tested. The more people get tested, the more likely you are to find a relative out there. Please keep an open mind when engaging in this type of testing. I get incredibly frustrated when people say, "Oh, I don't have any ancestry in those towns, therefore I can't be related to you," or, "I don't know any of those surnames. Our relative-finder match must have been a mistake."

There are no mistakes with DNA unless the company somehow mixed up your sample (which you would notice right away). If DNA says you have a lot in common with, for example, Italian groups, then maybe one of your ancestors came from Italy during Medieval or Roman times. It is possible. Keep an open mind and be willing to interact with other like-minded people across the globe.

The pros of DNA testing far outweigh the cons. Discovering ancestry beyond the paper trail is exhilarating and exciting. The results need to be taken with a grain of salt, but they are worth the money. DNA testing is the wave of the future, and every genealogist needs to catch the wave.

CHAPTER FOURTEEN: LIVING RELATIVES

I tell people that genealogical research is a team sport. It can be done independently, but seeking other people researching your family will produce a richer family tree than anyone can achieve on his or her own. The Ancestry website has a wonderful feature that allows its users to leave comments on individual records. I have left a comment for all lines of my family on many of its records so that if someone searched for them, he or she would see my comment and (hopefully) contact me. This is a good route to take for those who do not want their family trees posted on the Internet for everyone to see (and possibly steal credit from your hard work).

A. Other Genealogists

Search through the genealogy sites to find other members researching your ancestors and relatives. Contact them. If they posted on a genealogy site, then the odds are good that they want to be contacted and want to talk about family history. This really could open doors for your research. Do not hesitate; contact them!

B. Distant Relatives

Searching for relatives who are also researching your ancestors is the easy part. Contacting people who have never visited a genealogy website or attended a family history seminar is more difficult. I do not advise against it; in fact, I highly recommend trying to find relatives who are still alive. However, please exercise caution. Many people do not understand genealogy. They do not understand why we sift through old records to find information about people who died long before we were born. They think we are after money and trying to take advantage of them. Keep this in mind and be sure to clearly state your purpose and reassure relatives that this is definitely not the case.

I have done my share of contacting and have received some wonderful things in return. I have also received some bad things. Most of the time, I receive nothing. I have sent letters and called distant relatives, usually getting no response. However, it was that handful of wonderful people that I met that keep me going and convince me that there are good people who want to help others discover their shared ancestry.

How Can I Find Distant Cousins Who Are Still Alive?

1. Chart the collateral branches of your family. In other words, use the U.S. census records to chart the siblings of your direct ancestors along with their respective children and grandchildren. Get the most recently released census documents to research these people as close to present day as possible.
2. Search for the obituaries of the people who were alive in 1930. This sounds like a morbid second step, but obituaries are treasure troves of living people genealogy. I know that I was listed in several obituaries because grandchildren are often named in obituaries, especially if there aren't too many. Search for the people in the obituaries. For Cook County ancestry, use the Chicago Tribune or the Chicago Sun Times.

3. Use the people-finding tools offered on the Internet to find people that you could not find in obituaries as well as the people who were in the obituaries. www.zabasearch.com www.123people.com and www.intellius.com are excellent resources for finding living people.

4. Once you have found some people, pick out a few. Choose people who had the greatest connection to your ancestors. My first choice to contact lived with my gg-grandparents during the 1930 census and was still alive today. She is a wonderful woman of whom I hold in high regard. She shared some wonderful stories about my gg-grandparents that I never would have known. She remembered my grandmother and great aunt as well. Try to find the people who would know your relatives and use that avenue to explain to them who you are.

Write a short, succinct, and respectful letter as a way to contact distant relatives. Plainly explain your intent and how you are related to them. Give them all of your contact information. Suggest that they respond to you with a good time when you can call them. I have tried calling people out of the blue, but that has not gotten me good results.

Brace for the worst but hope for the best. It can be done, and it may produce some truly spectacular results. Without these techniques, my family tree would be a lot less interesting.

CHAPTER FIFTEEN: RESEARCH TIPS

During the course of my research, I have stumbled across some random facts about Polish–American genealogy. These don't fit in elsewhere, so this section has random suggestions that may help with your research.

Research the Siblings

When I first began genealogy, I made the mistake of thinking that genealogy is all about finding the direct ancestors and ignoring the rest. The practice of genealogy is so much richer and fuller by researching the entire family tree and that includes collateral lines. Some genealogists go so far as to find the siblings of all of their ancestors and then trace those siblings' descendants down to the present day.

It can be difficult to do this when Polish church records are scattered across a dozen rolls of microfilm, but it is easy to do this using American records and www.ancestry.com. I urge you to research your ancestors' siblings and their families as well. This is because people are not static. People change jobs, move around, get re-married, and so on. If you only focus on what your ggg-grandfather was like at the birth of your gg-grandfather, then you do not have the full picture of either of your ancestors. The Polish baptism records of all of your ggg-grandfather's children will paint the complete picture of him. Perhaps he started out as *wloscian*, peasant farmer, but worked hard in life and eventually purchased a farm of his own and became a *gospodarz* at the birth of his final child.

Finding siblings' birth records can also help break through brick walls that are inherent to genealogical research. I am researching the family of Antoni Pietrzak, who was born in approximately 1740 in Poland. The child of his that I am descended from is Augustus Pietrzak, who was born in 1772, but it was the birth record of Augustus' brother, Matthew, in 1769 that showed that Antoni Pietrzak's wife was Marianna, daughter of Thomas Kaminski. No other baptism record from that family showed the name of their grandfather. I never would have known the name of my gggggg-grandfather without that sibling's baptism record.

Although these people are not your direct ancestors, they certainly lived with and knew your ancestors. Even as lines drifted apart through the ages, they may still retain memories of their distant cousins. My grandmother still remembers the names of distant cousins on her line even if she could not remember how they are related to her. It pays off to research the siblings and their children because it just adds that wonderful layer of depth to your family tree.

Radom, Illinois

One research question that plagued me in my early days was what happened to Lorenz Mroz. According to the 1880 census, my gg-grandparents were living next door to my gg-grandmother's brother, Ignatz Jozwiak. He in turn was living with his mother, Marianna Janoska, his step-father, Frank Mroz, and Frank Mroz' brother Lorenz. I had been wracking my brain (and my keyboard) trying to figure out when Frank Mroz and my ggg-grandmother came to America and hoped that Lorenz was the key to finding an immigration record.

As stated in the previous section, I turned to Frank's sibling to see whether I could find his siblings' information. That was the biggest brick wall I ever faced. The man literally falls off the Cook County records after 1880. Before then, he was listed in church records as a godparent, found in city directories, and of course in the 1880 census. After that 1880 census, he disappears without a trace. I thought he either fell off the face of the earth or moved back to Poland.

As time passed, I gave up on finding Lorenz. I researched other branches and other people until I decided to restart the search for him. It said in the 1880 census that he was divorced, which I knew was almost impossible. Polish Catholics of this era rarely got divorced. The only divorces that I have seen among Polish Catholics were in cases of physical abuse (accompanied by chronic drunkenness) on the part of the husband, and the wife divorced him for her and her children's protection. It was possible that this happened, but I just didn't get that feeling. I thought something else was up.

An idea suddenly occurred to me. What if when the census taker asked his marital status, Lorenz said he was "separated" from his wife, as in she was elsewhere at the time, but the census taker thought he meant he was divorced? I got the feeling Lorenz didn't actually live in Chicago; maybe he was there just for a few months to earn some money. That got my adrenaline rushing, and I turned once again to my trusty PGSA website. Armed with that knowledge, I did another search for him and was startled to see that it had been updated with information from Washington County, Illinois. Lo and behold, Lawrence Mroz married Mary Musial in Radom, Illinois, in 1878. I had a great feeling about this, but as a good genealogist must, I consulted the original source on www.familysearch.org and received confirmation that this was my relative.

I know that was a long story, but I told it to share a relatively unknown factoid among the Polish in Chicago. Many genealogists, myself included, do not know that there was a large Polish population in Southern Illinois in Washington and Jefferson counties. In fact, the town of Radom was founded for the sole purpose of attracting Eastern Europeans to come to Illinois to farm it.

I actually discovered quite a few familiar surnames as I began browsing through the church books of the Diocese of Belleville. These images are online and free to access after registering with LDS on www.familysearch.org. I have just begun to research other people living there, but I have discovered that some of the early settlers of Chicago (1860s to 1870s era) travelled south to return to their first profession of farming as opposed to industry as the majority of Poles did. I actually found that a number of the early parishioners of St. Adalbert Church on the South Side lived in Southern Illinois by the 1880s.

In fact, if your ancestors were farmers, try searching for them on the U.S. Bureau of Land Management's website:
http://www.glorecords.blm.gov/search/default.aspx#searchTabIndex=0&searchByTypeIndex=0. If your ancestors purchased land patents early on from the government, then they may be listed here.

If you have relatives who settled early on in Chicago but fall of the map after that, check the records of Southern Illinois, because they may have taken up their ancestral calling to head back to the fields to farm.

Western Illinois

There was a large enclave of Polish-Americans in LaSalle County, Illinois, at the turn of the twentieth century. Many Ellis Island-era Poles were attracted to the manufacturing springing up in the area and settled in towns such as Ottawa, Peru, and LaSalle. Poles from all partitions lived there, but many from the Austrian partition were attracted there. Do not limit your searches to Cook County when researching Illinois ancestry; there may be other lines in other parts of Illinois.

Beyond Chicago

Keep in mind that our ancestors were like those today. Some people like staying in one place while others like to move from place to place. Many Poles headed west in the twentieth century, especially in the 1940s and 1950s. If you cannot find a death record for your ancestor in Illinois records, try California records for this time period. The California Death Index (http://vitals.rootsweb.ancestry.com/ca/death/search.cgi) hosted on Rootsweb is great for this. In fact, the nice thing about this database is that it lists both the surname and mother's maiden name of the deceased, so it is almost certain who exactly that person is in the death index.

Many of the older families of Chicago's Polonia, those who came in the 1860s and 1870s, moved onward to California in the middle of the twentieth century. Some did this for the economic opportunities found in the booming state. However, others did this for health reasons. My great-grandfather's niece, Janina Kruszka, moved to California because she needed a warm, dry climate for a chronic respiratory problem.

Also, many older folks retired in southern states from the 1960s onward. When they died, they usually had an obituary in the Chicago Tribune or Sun Times, especially if they still had family here, but not always. After checking the Social Security Death Index, check what death records are available for the state where your ancestor died. Retiring to Florida, Arizona, or Texas was (and still is) common.

Saints' Days and Naming Custom in Poland

Polish genealogy books like to talk about the old Polish naming customs. Although this information is interesting, sadly, it is not much help to genealogists. It is important to be aware of these customs, but do not put too much stock in them.

In Poland, there were two customs when it came to naming a newborn child. One was to name a child after a saint who had a feast day on or near that child's date of birth or baptism. When I say on or near, it could be on the exact day of birth or a few weeks into the future. It was not strict at all. I have found this custom in some of my ancestors but not the majority. If there are any unusual names in your family tree, look to see if the saint with that name had a feast day near the birth of your relative. Here is a helpful calendar   that   shows   the   saints   by   calendar   day: http://www.behindthename.com/namedays/lists/pol.php

The other custom was for the first-born son of the family to be named after the paternal grandfather while the second-born son was named after the father. This has been the more common custom in my family tree.

Exercise caution with both systems. The first rule of genealogy is not to make assumptions. Just because Paul Nowak named his first son Joseph does not mean that his father was named that or that Joseph was born on the feast day of St. Joseph. Simply keep these customs in mind as you scan your tree and wonder why your ancestors had the names that they did.

Church Books versus Duplicates

For all partitions, two copies of vital records were kept, one copy for the civil or state authorities and another for the religious authorities. In the Austrian and Russian partitions, the priest acted as both civil and religious record-keeper. Therefore, two copies were made of church documents. In the Prussian partition, the priest acted in both capacities until the Prussian government mandated civil, secular record-keeping in 1874.

I mention this as both a word of hope and a word of caution. The word of hope is that two copies were kept of your ancestors' vital records. Often, the originals were destroyed in war or acts of nature, so we only have the duplicates in existence for many parishes (many of mine included). Yes, that is good. However, the word of caution is that I have found many mistakes in duplicate records in comparison to the originals. Usually it is nothing big, such as the misnaming of a child. However, I have seen many village names and surnames misspelled as they were transcribed.

In fact, for the parish of Juncewo, the original records were kept in beautiful, neat handwriting whereas the duplicates are scrawled, sloppy, and illegible in parts. Imagine how disheartened I was when I first began my research on that family line with the duplicates!

I say this as a reminder to always access the original records when possible, but if those do not exist, exercise caution with the duplicates. If those are the only records left, then our only choice is to use those.

Remarriages

During my research, I found that almost every time a father or mother died when a small child was still alive, the surviving spouse remarried soon after. However, if all of their children were grown, then rarely did that spouse remarry. If parents got remarried after their spouses died, they would do so quickly, within two or three years, usually just one year, of their spouse's death.

Remember, in the eighteenth and nineteenth centuries, there really was no concept of "love" in a marriage in rural Poland. Marriages were done to economically link people and families together, and it really was not possible for a single-parent household to raise a child in that type of community. If it was just the father, then he was in the fields all day and unable to look after the child. If it was just the mother, then the family would have no income short of what others gave them. I imagine that people felt affection for their spouses, but remarriage and acceptance of death was just as much a part of Polish culture as *kiolbassa* and *pierogis* are. However, I did notice that after my gggg-grandfather, Jacob Gabrys, remarried, he named their first-born child after his first wife. I like to think that he did that because he loved her and wanted to remember her.

Another time to think about remarriages is when looking at marriage records. No, not the official records of the remarriage, but the marriage records of the children born to the original married couple. Sometimes the child would put down the new spouse as their parent on marriage records. That really threw me when I first began researching. Apparently, it was done as a show of respect for the living person who, theoretically, cared for them when their biological parent had died and could not.

This was the case of Thomas Szarzynski, a relative by marriage. I found his marriage record in Chicago, and he listed Joseph Szarzynski and Frances Chmiel as his parents. I was excited because Frances Chmiel was my gg-grandmother's sister. However, my heart sank when I found Thomas' baptism record in Trzemeszno in 1869 and saw that his birth mother was Catherine Magowska. She died when he was three years old, and his father remarried my ancestor's sibling soon after that. He probably had no memory of his birth mother and therefore considered Frances his mother although biologically she was not.

Tips for Searching

A. Steve Morse Website

I always laugh when I read genealogy books that say how easy it is to find records once you know your ancestor's full names. Maybe that is true for Americana names such as "John Smith" and "James Thompson" but rarely for "Wojciech Nowaczyk" or "Wawrzyniec Wyborski." If you are Polish, get ready to spend more time sifting through online results than your Americana friends. And that is OK. It all comes with being Polish.

A useful website that can help to search certain websites is http://www.stevemorse.org/. Steve Morse created this website that allows for more freedom and flexibility with your search queries in certain sites such as the vital records database on www.cyberdriveillinois.com. He also created searches for fields that were indexed but are not searchable. Cyber Drive does not allow searches for the date of a death record although it was transcribed. Steve Morse's clever search engine allows just that.

Something else that his site has is the enumeration district finder for the 1900 through 1940 censuses. See Chapter Two on how to use this tool to find a particular address in census records.

B. Mocavo

Mocavo is a new search engine that searches genealogical websites for key words and phrases. The website is small but growing and has the potential to be a fantastic resource once its scope is expanded: http://mocavo.com/

Facebook

Millions of people around the world use Facebook to connect and interact with other people. Some of those people are genealogists who have set up Facebook groups dedicated to some facet of genealogy. A Facebook group is a collection of users who share a common page dedicated to a particular subject. The PGSA has its own group page as does Ancestry, Family Search, and many other genealogical organizations. To find these pages, type the name of the organization in the search bar at the top of the screen, and if that organization has a group page, it will pop up in the search results.

There are also individuals who run Facebook groups dedicated to some facet of genealogy such as a particular village, surname, or clan. One such group is called "Descendants of Osobnica" and is used to connect with other people who have ancestry in the Polish village of Osobnica. I created a Facebook group dedicated to my Jozwiak ancestors in the hope that another person related to my Jozwiak family will find the page and connect with me that way.

Anyone can create a Facebook group, and there are thousands of Facebook groups dedicated in some way, shape, or form to genealogy. It is definitely worth a shot to try to connect with other people who share your ancestry or are also interested in genealogy. Like I said before, genealogy is a team sport, and the more people involved, the better the team will be.

Conclusion

I said at the beginning of this book that I did not intend it to be an encyclopedia or a reference work compiling every little facet of Polish–American genealogy, although it feels like that to me! This was intended as a guidebook and a compendium of useful strategies for finding your Polish ancestors in Cook County and beyond.

I hope you enjoyed this book, and I would love to hear feedback from you. Feel free to email any genealogy questions you have to me at: kruskij@gmail.com

The purpose of this book is to help others. Genealogy is a team sport. We need to help each other discover our ancestry, and when we do, I believe the world will be a richer, brighter place. Thank you for reading my book, and I wish you the very best of luck in your genealogical quest.

APPENDICES

Appendix A: Websites of Interest to Chicago Polish

Over the course of this book, I have referenced websites that are essential resources for genealogists conducting Polish genealogical research in Cook County. Here is a list for ease with a summary of what is found at each one. I give more detailed insight into each website in the appropriate chapters. The websites are listed in order of usefulness to genealogists.

1. **www.ancestry.com**: The bread and butter of every genealogist. All U.S. census records, ship manifests, some vital records, military documents, and much more are found on this wonderful site. I strongly urge all genealogists to purchase a subscription to this site in the beginning of a genealogical search because it gives the resources needed to take your Polish family tree back as far as possible in the United States and even a little further than that. It is well worth the money, and you will never regret it. This site also gives the opportunity to become an indexer who helps create searchable Internet databases of old records. See "Community—World Archives Project" for more details.

2. **www.familysearch.org**: This is the website of the Church of Latter Day Saints (LDS). They have collected records from all over the world from a wide variety of sources ranging from funeral home records to census records to military enlistment registrars. This site's utility has increased exponentially over time. Visit it often, I recommend at least once a week, because new records are uploaded at a tremendous pace. There are many Cook County resources along with the transcribed death index for all of Illinois from 1916 to 1947. This site also has an indexing program, to which I actively contribute. The difference between this site and Ancestry is that it is entirely free. The majority of databases are searchable as a free guest, and the rest can be searched by registering with the site. LDS has given the world of personal genealogy an immeasurable gift with its decades of work preserving the past. Honor this work by visiting their website and helping them turn the dream of family history into a reality for millions around the globe.

3. **www.pgsa.org**: This is the website of the Polish Genealogical Society of America, the foremost (in my opinion) Polish genealogical society. It is a veritable diamond mine of resources for Polish genealogists in Cook County. It contains information—such as obituaries from a prominent Polish paper in Chicago, indexes of Jubilee Books, and marriage records from Chicago churches—not found anywhere else on the Internet. The site also has some nice links about Poland and Polish culture. It is a great resource for all Polish–American genealogists.

4. **www.rootsweb.com**: An extremely useful resource for researchers in the early 2000s is now more of a novelty site for researchers. It started out as an excellent resource for genealogists but has since fallen into disuse in favor of Ancestry. However, it still contains a lot of good information, especially if someone has posted a family tree that includes your relatives. Also, the Social Security Death Index on this site is the best one I

have used. There are some interesting links about Poland and its different regions. There was once an indexing project for Polish records, but little has changed in the past few years. Then again, if your parish was indexed, that would be truly spectacular.

5. **www.cyberdriveillinois.com**: Click on "Services" in the upper-left corner then "Government Records" then "Genealogical Resources" then "Databases" and everything that the State of Illinois has to offer for genealogists pops up. Illinois actually has a lot to offer genealogists, much more than many other states. The most useful databases for Chicago Polish are the Early Illinois Marriages Index and the two Illinois Deaths databases. Check out the other databases, too, especially the Illinois military databases.

6. **www.ellisisland.org** and **www.castlegarden.org**: These are the two best sites on the web for finding ship records, aside from Ancestry, of course. Both sites are totally free to use but ask for donations to their respective noble causes. The difference is that the Ellis Island site has the images accompanying their transcriptions whereas Castle Garden does not. The Ellis Island site is useful for the later wave of Poles to Cook County, mainly those from the Russian and Austrian partitions. The Ellis Island site covers the years of Ellis Island from 1892 until the mid-1920s. Their search engine is rather clumsy and does not do a good job of searching for alternate spellings. That being said, this site is still a valuable resource for genealogists. Plus, it is free. The Castle Garden site covers when Castle Garden was the immigration station for those coming into New York City from 1855 until 1890 along with some data from other years. The official time frame of the website is from 1820 to 1913. The majority of records are from the mid-1800s. However, Castle Garden is much less useful because it does not have the images online and has indexed a much smaller percentage of the record span in comparison to the Ellis Island site. Both sites can be great assets when searching for relatives, and when used in conjunction with Ancestry and Family Search, are great tools for genealogists.

7. **www.cookcountygenealogy.com/**: This is a commercial website set up by Cook County to sell copies of birth, marriage, and death certificates from its massive warehouses. The old-fashioned way of ordering a record was to fill out a form issued by Cook County, mail in payment (probably in the form of a check or money order), wait a few weeks, and then receive a paper copy in the mail that has been folded and stamped with "FOR GENEALOGICAL PURPOSES ONLY." This website allows the instant download of any vital record that has been posted on it. The fee is the same as the old-fashioned way, plus a small surcharge for ordering online. Many of these records can be found for free on www.familysearch.org. However, not all are. This website is especially useful for recent records (1930s to 1950s), which have the greatest coverage. The county is slowly adding its resources to this site. It is by no means a complete database. However, I applaud Cook County for putting together this website. Few other counties in the United States have a system like this. There is some limited information such as when your ancestors married and to whom. If you know their names and the time span, the later the year the more likely the record will appear on the site. Few early records are online, but again, this is a work in progress. Registration for this site is free, so it is definitely worth a visit.

8. **www.cookcountyclerkofcourt.org/NR/:** This is a project started by the Cook County Court system to index the declarations of intent filed in Cook County from 1906 to 1929. The beauty of this particular database is that it has virtually all useful information transcribed from each record it has processed. It even includes the declarant's address and village of origin. The best part about this is that these are all searchable fields with the controls on the sidebar on the left side of the screen. It is useful to see who was naturalized at which address, and you may find some hidden relatives by searching only a city rather than a name. This collection is not complete and is looking for volunteers. Hopefully with time, this will grow into a fantastic resource.

9. **http://chicagoancestors.org/:** This site was created by the Newberry Library staff. It has some useful links along with copies of Chicago city directories in full form to browse through. These are useful when used in conjunction with census records and other types of information.

10. **www.nara.gov:** I feel obligated to mention the website of the National Archives of the United States because it has great information about the various records of the federal government. It has instructions on how to order military records and forms to fill out to perform records searches. The best database that it has is the World War II enlistment records database that. Ancestry does not have this information, so it is a useful database for doing recent ancestral research.

11. **www.google.com** and **www.wikipedia.org:** Google and Wikipedia are excellent resources for genealogists— I am not joking. They may not help with researching a Ph.D. dissertation, but they are great for finding information quickly. The days of sifting through dusty maps and papers at genealogy libraries are nearing an end, I am afraid. Poland has not entirely embraced the Internet yet, so it does not have the volume of material online that other countries have. That being said, there is still a lot of excellent information online.

I have included many other websites scattered throughout this book, but the above websites will help with the bulk of your research. It is up to you to discover smaller sites that can help you. One such site is that of Dr. Jay Orbik (http://www.orbikfamily.com/). This is a wonderful resource for Chicago history and a model for how to go about your research. There are countless other useful websites for Polish–American genealogists. Go out there and find them!

Appendix B: Tips for Searching Internet Databases

A common mistake that I see beginning genealogists make is that they search for their ancestors using their ancestors' exact names and birthdates in Internet databases such as Ancestry and Family Search. They then get frustrated because the census record that they need does not pop up. I then modify the search terms a bit, and the record shows up eventually. They gasp in wonder and ask how I found them although their information was correct.

Here's a tip: You know the information of your ancestors, but the census takers did not. They may have recorded the correct surname but wrong first name. They may have misheard your ancestor and wrote 1860 as year of birth instead of 1870. Therefore, for Polish genealogy, do not make specific searches for specific names and years, for example

Change around the search terms. If you cannot find your ancestor by first name or surname, try using other search terms in a vague, generic search. Ancestry's index is wonderful because terms other than the person's name can be used to find people. For example, a useful technique is to use information other than the name in the search box. Say your ancestor was born in 1855, mark that and a two-year range in the birth field, along with "Chicago" in the keyword box, and give the birthplace as "Poland" or "Prussia." That will give many results to sift through, which might be your ticket to an early census record.

A "starting with" search can be useful for long Polish surnames such as Andrzejewski. Do this type of search on the LDS website by typing an asterisk (*) at the end of your search entry that contains the first few letters of the surname. A birth certificate from 1890 probably will not have "Andrzejewski" spelled correctly, but it probably will have the first few letters. Search for the child's surname with "Andr*" at first or "And*" along with some other search fields to try to find that record.

Personal names can be tricky, especially for English-speaking clerks who did not understand how the Polish language works. Try searching for someone via their year of birth, residence in Chicago, and birthplace. Leave the name fields blank. Yes, that may give hundreds of search results, but if one of those is the correct one, wasn't that search worth it?

Or, try typing in the full name of your ancestor and nothing else. If the needed record does not pop up, try different combinations of different information. The LDS website has fields for a child's first and last names along with the first and last names of their parents and year of birth. Use those fields in different combinations.

To find an elusive birth certificate for my great-grandmother's sister, I had to try everything. Her name was Pelagia Pietrzak. Nothing worked, not even an only-mother's maiden name search, until finally I simply entered in her mother's first name and a year span. Luckily her mother had the fairly unusual name Constance and thus I did not have to sift through thousands of entries like I would have if her name was Mary. I tried "Constance" to no luck but tried the Polish version "Konstancia," and lo and behold, I found it. Using this same technique I found birth records for two more siblings' who had died as infants.

Try using different bits of information and different spellings. Ancestry has a more flexible search box, so it is easier to mix and match specific pieces of information on there than on Family Search. However, get creative with search strings. Always give a range for birth year and remember that correct spelling on a personal name on an American document from the nineteenth century is the exception and not the rule. Get creative and give it your all when performing searches in online databases.

Appendix C: Locations of Interest to Chicago Research

1. Home Computer

The age of sitting in stuffy rooms with microfilm readers and bending over census records is over. Today, the majority of genealogical records are found online in some shape or form. The best tool for genealogical research today is a reliable and fast computer and a high-speed Internet connection. You cannot hope to advance in your genealogy if you do not have these resources easily at your disposal. The best place of interest to Polish–American researchers is the Internet. See Appendix A for specific websites that are of the most interest to genealogists. If you do not have a computer with Internet access or it is not working properly, then visit your local public library to use their computers.

2. Local LDS Family History Center

After exhausting what the Internet holds for your ancestors, it is time to begin pushing your family tree beyond the shores of America and back to the mysterious lands of Poland. The resources that LDS has to offer will help accomplish this. Find out which Polish church books and other Polish records have been microfilmed. Not many Polish records have made it online to www.familysearch.org so this research will need to be done the old-fashioned way—in a library with a microfilm reader.

Go to the LDS website and find a family history library that is close to your home; they are scattered across the United States so you should be able to find one. The two main ones in the Chicago area are the Waukegan and Naperville libraries, both of which have excellent Chicago resources and facilities that are wonderful to use.

I am most familiar with the Naperville Library; I go there a few times a month. They have a full collection of Catholic Church books for Chicago including all of the Polish parishes needed in Chicago. Waukegan has this collection, too. The staff is friendly and will help with your research if you come prepared with information.

To view the church books that LDS has microfilmed, order the roll with that particular church book. Find out which roll by searching for the locality in the library catalog of the LDS website. Order microfilm in one of two ways. The first way is to bring that information to the library and ask for a film request form. Fill out the form and pay the small fee, usually six dollars, to cover shipping. This is the old fashioned way of ordering. The second way to order films is online via https://www.familysearch.org/films/ which is the only way to order for some LDS libraries. Go to that site and follow the instructions in order to place an order online, which currently is $5.50 for a short-term loan of microfilm.

The main library in Salt Lake City will then mail a copy of that microfilm roll to your local family history center for research. It can take as little as two weeks; it can take as long as a few months. Be patient. The period of time that the film will be at your library is up to your library, but it is plenty of time to peruse and research that film.

The rest is up to you. Order as many films as you need to research your family. Getting used to microfilm is easy, and once you have mastered the art of fiddling with the knobs and levers of each individual microfilm reader in your library (trust me, each microfilm reader has its own quirks), then you will be ready to journey deep into the mists of time.

3. Cook County Complex—Richard J. Daley Center

This collection of buildings houses the records needed to trace your ancestors' Cook County ancestry. Most of this information is online, but it is still worth a trip to downtown Chicago to research probate and obtain original copies of naturalization documents. It is also useful to travel to the complex to purchase vital records not found on any of the online indexes.

I had to find the death certificate of my gg-grandmother's brother, Michael Mazgaj, who died in South Chicago in 1953. His death information was elusive, but I found a death entry for someone of the same name in 1953. I ordered that death certificate in person and was thankful that I did because his name was listed as "Mike" not "Michael." This isn't a big deal for genealogists, but for city employees who like things to be exact, this is a big deal. If I wasn't there to explain that "Mike Mazgaj" is the same person as "Michael Mazgaj" I believe my request would have been returned with a "no record found" certificate.

Do a web search for the location of the "Cook County Clerk" the "Cook County Assessor's Office" and "Cook County Circuit Court Archives" to obtain detailed information about their hours and locations. These are the three main locations in the Cook County complex that can help in a genealogical search.

4. Cemeteries—St. Adalbert and Resurrection

Visiting the place of burial for your ancestors is definitely a plus. St. Adalbert is the main cemetery for North Side Polish to be buried, and Resurrection is the main cemetery for South Side Polish. Try your research at one of those locations based on where your ancestors lived. Then search the automated kiosk in the lobby of each of these cemeteries to find exactly where in the cemetery (or which Catholic cemetery) your ancestor was buried.

Cemeteries do not have detailed records about these people. The best they can do is look up a particular person in their ledger books to see who else is buried in that person's burial plot and their respective dates of death.

I recommend taking a photograph of your ancestors' graves to help remember where in the cemetery they are located. Bring some basic garden tools to clear away debris around the headstone. Also, look at the graves around your ancestors' because people were often buried near their relatives. Visiting these cemeteries can add a new layer to your family history research and is the last way to say hello to one of your ancestors. See Chapter Six for more information about cemetery research.

5. Illinois Regional Archives Depository (IRAD)—Northeastern Illinois University

The IRAD system is the archival system for the state of Illinois. It has a branch at the state universities in Illinois, and each branch covers a different region of the state.

The records held at each branch vary from county to county, so it pays to call ahead before making a trip.

The records of Cook County are held in the IRAD branch at Northeastern Illinois University. What kinds of records? Well, they have a little bit of everything from city directories to birth indexes to liquor licenses. It really is too much to list here; this information can be found on the Cyberdrive website previously listed. It's also worth a call to talk to a person. The staff there is friendly, and they don't get too many visitors in a day so they can spend time assisting your search.

Appendix D: Recommended Readings

1. *God's Playground: A History of Poland*, Volumes 1 and 2, by Norman Davies

I said at the beginning of this book that reading a history of Poland would be extremely beneficial to genealogists. Understanding what was happening at the time our ancestors lived is absolutely fascinating. It can also help explain why our ancestors acted in the way they did. My Mazgaj and Iglewski family moved from the Prussian partition to the Russian partition some time between 1871 and 1874. Understanding the *Kulturkampf* and what it meant for the Poles living through it helped me understand why they would do that. Davies has done Poles around the globe a wonderful service by writing this magnificent work. His Anglo-Saxon surname may cast doubt upon first glance at this book, but this man truly knows what Poland is and what it means to be Polish. He details the history of Poland from ancient times to the rise of the Polish–Lithuanian Commonwealth to the partitioning of Poland to World War II to the rise of the country that Poland is today. I have never read a better book about the history of Poland, and I highly recommend both volumes for anyone interested in its.

2. *The Polish Way: A Thousand-Year History of the Poles and Their Culture* by Adam Zamoyski

This is another excellent tome on the history of Poland. It is more condensed than Davies' book and is written by a descendant of the ancient Zamoyski magnate family of Poland. It details the history of Poland from its birth in 966 until the twentieth century. It is written in a fluid manner that is both entrancing and easy to read. Zamoyski devotes much time to the formative years of the Polish–Lithuanian Commonwealth and does an excellent job showing the contribution that Poland made to the arts. This was an excellent book and is a nice compliment to Davies' more comprehensive history.

3. *Going Home: A Guide to Polish–American Family History Research* by Jonathan Shea

This is the single best book I have read on the subject of personal Polish–American family history research. Shea has a guide that exhausts resources both on this side of the Atlantic and the other side. His book is filled with useful tidbits and helpful suggestions on how to proceed with your research. He is a language professor, so naturally he includes a great section about the intricate nature of the Polish language along with translation guides. This book will help a great deal for researching your Polish ancestors across the United States but especially in the Northeastern states. I applaud Shea on his work and highly recommend it to genealogy beginners and experts alike.

4. *Polish Roots* by Rosemary Chorzempa

This Polish–American family history guide was wonderful and helpful when starting my research. Chorzempa sought to create a book that breaks down Polish–American genealogy into something useful and approachable to genealogists of all levels.

It has helpful sections that detail the different records available here along with information on little-known sources of information. I consider it and Shea's work to be the two best books produced in the field of Polish–American genealogy.

Other Books

I have read dozens of books in the fields of genealogy and Polish history, and the previously mentioned four books are the best I have encountered. I have found that books written specifically toward Polish genealogy are the best as opposed to the book series sponsored by Ancestry, which covers all nationalities. There are some books dedicated to a particular facet of genealogy such as *They Came in Ships* by John Colletta (immigration records) and *They Became Americans* by Lou Szucs (naturalization records). Although these are interesting to read, I recommend conducting your own genealogy first and then turn to books such as these to help answer questions you have. Use these reference books for help when stuck on a particular record that you have found, and do not start your search by reading this book.

Appendix E: My Genealogy

These Polish surnames are on my direct line:

Kruszka/Kruszki/Kruski, Mazgaj, Lewandowski, Iglewski/Igla, Wyborski, Cichowlas, Soltysiak, Trusch, Stefaniak, Nowak, Kaminski, Pijanowski/Pilarski, Jozwiak, Janoski/Janusziak/Januszewski, Bara, Brongiel/Bragiel, Ulaszek, Byczek, Dybas, Kosiek, Kaczor, Macuga, Zydek, Gliwa, Budziak, Stelmach, Dubka, Padiasek, Smola/Smolak, Kedzierski, Gabrys, Majerczak, Slowik, Weglarz, Jarzyna, Kliszor/Klyzsz/Kleszynski, Zofieja, Swieton/Jalen, Pietrzak, Chmiel/Chmielewski/Hoppe, Luczynski, Jerzewski, Paulus/Polus/Palus, Graczyk, Kozinski, Radki

These Polish surnames are related to me through marriage:

Rybowicz, Myslinski, Musial, Klebba, Kowalczyk, Burzynski, Kuzniecki, Mroz, Serba, Mondrala/Madrala, Ogrodowski, Topp, Cyranek, Zec, Bandosz, Kinowski, Borucki, Skoraczewski, Kudla, Marszalek, Bachta, Ciciora, Szafarz, Kapanowski, Lazar, Bartus, Watroba, Bartosiak, Borchman, Lenske, Mazurowski, Kowalski, Szarzynski, Jagodzinski

Even better than the surnames are the locations in Poland I can claim ancestry from. Even if you do not share any of the surnames listed above, I'd still love to talk to you if you have ancestry in one of these places. The marriage surnames reflect turn-of-the-century marriages of a few lines, not all of them. If we share a common village, then we probably share common ancestry at some point. If we put our brains (and family trees) together, I bet we can uncover something.

Places of Origin for My Family Divided by Partition

Prussian: Grabie, Inowroclaw, Poland (Grabie, Aleksandrow Kujawski, West Prussia); Niemczyn, Kozielsko, Poland; Starezyn, Juncewo, Poland; Piecki Małe, Strzelno, Poland; Skotniki Zabłotne, Strzelno, Poland; Paproć, Inowroclaw, Poland; Chawlodno, Czeszewo, Poland; Miedzyslisle, Znin, Poland; most of the villages around Trzemeszno, Mogilno, Poland; Kruchowo, Duszno, Poland

Russian: Stary Brzesc, Brzesc Kujawski, Wloclawek; Wies Katy, Wieniec, Poland; Lukowa, Bilgoraj, Poland; Olchowiec, Bilgoraj, Poland; Olsza, Bilgoraj, Poland; Wola Wapowska, Bilgoraj, Poland

Austrian: Szczawnica, Nowy Targ, Poland; Kroscienko, Nowy Targ, Poland; Osobnica, Jaslo, Poland

If you share any of these surnames or locations in your family tree, contact me at kruskij@gmail.com. Who knows? I may be your fourth cousin, twice removed, which would be awesome.

Appendix F: Bibliography and Note on Sources

This book reflects the original research and analysis performed by myself, Jason Kruski, in the realm of Polish–American genealogy in Cook County and in Poland. Therefore, the views, opinions, and analyses expressed in these pages are solely my own work based on my own research and in no way, shape, or form reflect the official viewpoints or positions held by Cook County, Ancestry, the Polish archives system, or any other official organization mentioned in this book. This is a guidebook based on the years of research I spent on my personal genealogy along with other genealogical work I have done for others.

That being said, my main sources of information are the records themselves. These are original documents not subjected to outside analysis other than my own, and they can be can be accessed in the places I said they would be found in their respective chapters.

Information about genetic genealogy and DNA in general was formulated after studying it in high school and college courses. A resource that influenced my views on genetic genealogy is:

Wells, Spencer. *Deep Ancestry: Inside the Genographic Project.* National Geographic, 2006. Print.

Information about vital record keeping in Illinois can be found at: http://www.cyberdriveillinois.com/departments/archives/serv_sta.html

As far as the historical background information provided, I purposely kept it minimal and spoke in general statements. This is a genealogical guidebook, not a historical textbook. Most of the information I stated can be considered common knowledge. To help me formulate my ideas about Polish history, I consulted:

Davies, Norman. *God's Playground: A History of Poland, Vol. 1: The Origins to 1795.* Columbia University Press, 2005. Print

Davies, Norman. *God's Playground: A History of Poland, Vol. 2: 1795 to the Present.* Columbia University Press, 2005. Print.

Zamoyski, Adam. *The Polish Way: A Thousand-Year History of the Poles and Their Culture.* Hippocrene Books, 1993. Print.

CPSIA information can be obtained at www.ICGtesting.com
Printed in the USA
BVOW021712250512

291133BV00005B/16/P